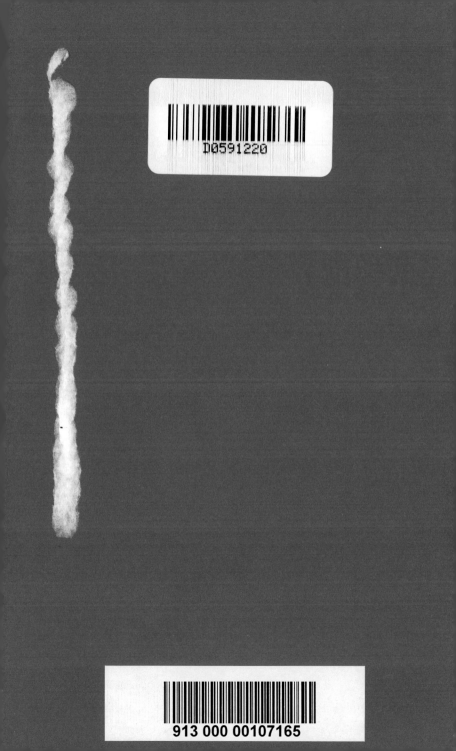

I love you
with
Custard on
top x

Also by Oonagh O'Hagan

I Lick My Cheese: And Other Notes
from the Frontline of Flatsharing

I love you with Custard on top x

AND OTHER NOTES
FROM THE WILDER SHORES OF
LOVE

Oonagh O'Hagan

sphere

Sphere

First published in Great Britain in 2010 by Sphere

Copyright © Oonagh O'Hagan 2010

Permission for the material used in this book has been applied for.

The moral right of the author has been asserted.

A CIP catalogue record for this book
is available from the British Library.

ISBN 978-1-84744-273-4

Page design by The Flying Fish Studios Ltd
Printed and bound in Italy

Papers used by Sphere are natural, renewable and recyclable
products sourced from well-managed forests and certified in
accordance with the rules of the Forest Stewardship Council.

Mixed Sources
Product group from well-managed
forests and other controlled sources
www.fsc.org   Cert no. SGS-COC-004081
© 1996 Forest Stewardship Council

FSC

Sphere
An imprint of
Little, Brown Book Group
100 Victoria Embankment
London EC4Y 0DY

An Hachette UK Company
www.hachette.co.uk

www.littlebrown.co.uk

Contents

1   **Foreword**

5   **Sowing the Seeds**
Hopeful Love
Feel Good Love
Creative Love
Euphoric Love

85   **The First Flush**
Saucy/Fetish Love
Obsessive Love

151   **A Turn for the Worse**
Reading Between the Lines of Love
Bad News and Lost Love
No Love/Hate

225   **Things Can Only Get Better and Happy Endings**
Long Distance Love
Sickly Sweet Love
Forgive and Forget Love
Selfless Love

271   **Afterword and Acknowledgements**

Foreword

Making love. A phrase that immediately makes me think of religious studies classes and drawings of bearded men and – frankly – destroys my libido.

So instead of 'making' love, let's talk about the making *of* love, and what it actually means. Does it mean friendship? Compromise? Commitment? No commitment? Being tied up, covered in rice pudding and beaten with a stick? However you define it, love seems to mean a lot to everyone. 'No it doesn't!' I hear you shout. 'I couldn't give a shit about love, I just want to do it. Do it, do it, do it.'

Doing it. Another phrase that I just can't take seriously. It makes me think of those nature programmes in which animals do a great deal of thrusting in a very short period of time, while looking curiously bored by the entire process. (Do animals fall in love? Or is the entire procreation process all about that quick, thrusting minute for them? And is there anything wrong with a quick thrusting minute anyway?)

In any event, animals get off lightly when it comes to searching for love. They have a whole array of fancy-pants moves and signals – dogs even have specific times of the year when all systems are go – but it's all quite simple to understand, I imagine. On the other hand, we humans have created endless and ever more complicated forms of communication with which to woo: talking, writing letters, and in recent years emailing and texting.*

And that is what this book is about: the way that we communicate our love.

I don't profess to be an expert on the topic, but it's clear that love

---

* Texting is not without its perils. With the invention of predictive text, it's become all too easy to mix up 'lips' with 'kiss', 'cock' with 'anal', or 'fuck' with 'dual'. Dangerous ...

means different things to different people. This book looks at love in all of its guises – from innocent childhood friendships, to teenage obsessions, to what can only be described as hot, wild-eyed *lust*. So I use the term 'love' notes in the broadest sense.

A lot of love has been spread around to make this book possible. I carried out my own research, of course, but I also bullied various friends into speed dating and looking for love online. You'll find smatterings from these eclectic experiences throughout, along with the notes I gathered from a variety of strange and wonderful sources. And not all of us are blessed with Mario Testino-like talent, judging by the quality of some of the images. Sorry! If you fancy spreading your love and possibly having it published, visit my website at www.flatmatesanonymous.com, where there's a whole section devoted to love notes. I'm still waiting for someone to propose on the site, so crack on with it!

After my last book on flatmates' notes,* I was occasionally asked whether the notes were real. Sometimes for scary legal reasons, and also because the book wasn't about naming and shaming people, we had to block out names and tweak bits of various notes to hide identities, but as far as I know they are real. Of course, it also depends what you mean by 'real' – I have no way of testing or finding out whether the events actually happened, and can't really do any scientific tests. (Let's face it, we aren't exactly trying to carbon date the Turin Shroud here.) The question of authenticity becomes even more amusing in the context of love notes. I quite like the idea of someone feverishly writing torrid love letters to themselves and then sending them to me. And before you start to get all disapproving on me, I found out that some of people's favourite notes from the last book were on the subject of 'self love' ...

* *I Lick My Cheese: And Other Notes from the Frontline of Flatsharing*

Sowing the Seeds

This chapter is about the time before a relationship has begun – the period during which the seeds are sown. Essentially it's all about potential. That initial twinge when you first say to yourself, 'Hold on, I feel a bit weird about this person.' It can happen after the briefest of encounters, or even in your imagination – it doesn't stop you wanting to be with that person. Of course, the potential for love can sometimes be more exciting than the reality, and I'm not just talking about the difference between humping an avatar in 'Second Life' and then discovering that, in *real* life, they're as physically and mentally exciting as a potato. The relationship might begin in your mind, but then perhaps you try to get the ball rolling by initiating contact – sending them gifts … or even writing a note. And it can be a great time – the thrill of the chase, the hoping, the wooing, the first date – a million miles away from the point at which the novelty wears off. So for now, let's venture into the giddy world of potential love …

HOPEFUL LOVE

Fingers, toes and eyes crossed!
These are the notes you write when you've plucked up
the courage to chance your arm and give it a go.
The sky's the limit!

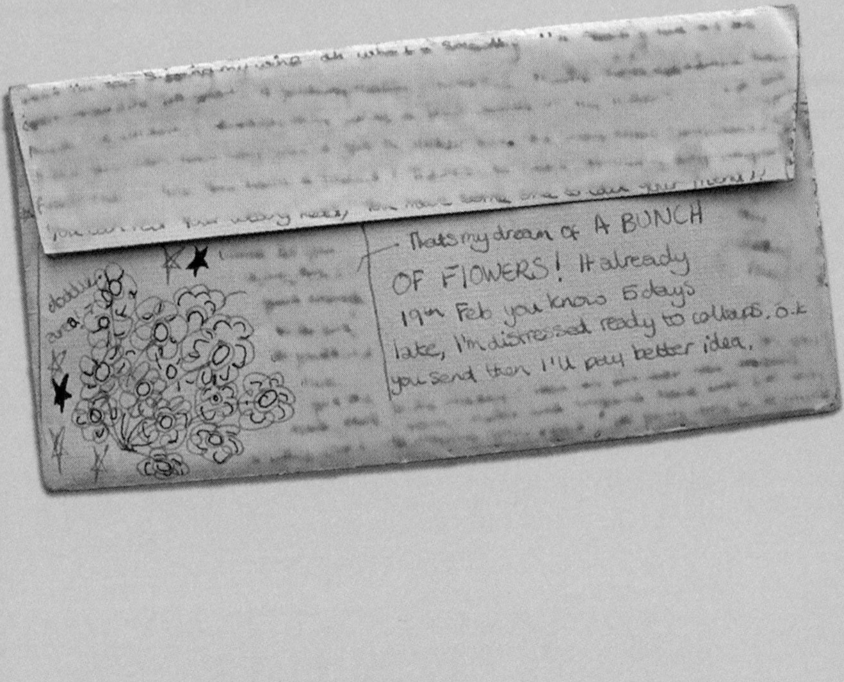
Thats my dream of A BUNCH
OF FLOWERS! It already
19th Feb you know 5 days
late, I'm distressed ready to collapse. o.k
you send then I'll pay better idea.

According to the Victorians different flowers meant different things. Lilies represented death, apple blossom meant kept promises … as we'll discover throughout this book, those bloody Victorians have a lot to answer for with all their repressed feelings and secret messages. One thing is clear, though: dead flowers are never a good sign. Receiving flowers can be a lovely experience, but for some reason whenever I get them, I panic. Have I forgotten an anniversary? Valentine's Day? My own birthday? Sadly, there's no such thing as an innocent gesture when it comes to bouquets, as invariably the recipient starts to wonder what's been going on. Are you cheating on me? Have you been sending flowers to someone else, too? Are you seeing the florist?

The idea of receiving flowers might be wonderful in theory, but the reality is that you'll be a gibbering wreck by the end of the day.

Dear   ,   14th, February 1997.

       Thank you for the Valentine card. I woke up this morning and my thoughts went straight to the notion that it was Valentine's Day and I said to myself that I had no effing chance of receiving a card from anyone. That was my thought and I was gobsmacked when I opened the envelope that was pushed through my postbox. It cheered me up no end. I do not get a lot of letters unless it is either junk mail or bills which everyone gets so as you can see it was something of an eye opener for me.

You don't need to be Lord Byron to pen beautiful prose, and although this isn't particularly sophisticated I think it's great. If you're ever in a quandary about sending a valentine, then this note (not to mention this book) shows you exactly why you should: it brought so much happiness and excitement to this person's day that they felt compelled to hit a word processor and write this. Hold on, who uses a word processor these days? This person maybe needs as much love as they can get …

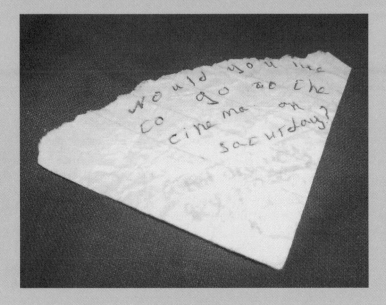

Is it just me or are people getting into relationships at a younger and younger age? This note looks like it was written by someone who's barely learned how to write, let alone date.

When I was a child I was far too busy drawing pictures and hanging out with my mum to think about boys (ugh). But with the arrival of pole-dancing kits for 'tweenagers' and high heels for babies (what's next, terry-towelling thongs for toddlers?), it's little wonder the dating game is being played earlier. OK, so I'm not suggesting parents should keep their offspring in arrested development for ever – a thermal vest tucked into Y-fronts is not a good look beyond the age of twenty-one – but surely giving a little girl nail extensions when she can't even tie her own shoelaces is über wrong? Hopefully they're only going to a U-rated movie …

If this is meant to plant steamy thoughts in the head of the recipient, leaving them gasping to see the sender, then I reckon it's failed. It just looks like a picture of that bloke from Right Said Fred, and there's nothing steamy about him.

Note Portfolio
Pochette de notes

10 NOTES (Blank Inside)
ENVELOPES
10 NOTES (sans texte à l'intérieur)
ENVELOPPES

©H
Kans,
MADE IN U.S.A.
www.hallmark.com

U.S.A
CP.

helo,
yeah it went well, but
remember not ta order sticky
no's on the first date
XXX

16

It's horrible eating in front of someone you like. You seem to lose all hand–eye coordination and the ability to remember the size of your mouth. You spend half the time bowed dutifully over your meal, chewing on an oversized lettuce leaf or some other poncy garnish you really should have shredded before eating. And when you nip to the loo, there it all is, lodged firmly between your teeth, like the canopy of the Amazon. Bollocks.

The trick is to chop everything into small pieces and pray they don't ask you something just as you put a really fucking hot piece of food in your mouth (regurgitating in front of a date generally leaves them cold). Or why not get everything puréed first, and try passing it off as some sort of LA diet? That said, a lot of men say they find women who watch what they eat unattractive. So why not just go for it? Swing that spaghetti round your head and fellate as many vegetables you can get your hands on …

FEEL GOOD LOVE

It only went and ruddy worked! You can practically hear
the contented sighs emanating from these love notes.
These are the good time letters that put a smile on your face.

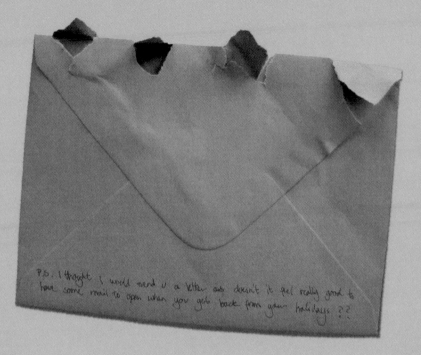

P.S. I thought I would send u a letter as doesn't it feel really good to have some mail to open when you get back from your holidays ??

Looking at life from someone else's point of view and trying to make that life better is one of the signs of a good relationship, and this note is a case in point. Coming back from a holiday is often a joyless experience, made even worse when you wedge open your front door to find that the only post behind it is an avalanche of bills and flyers from the local takeaway. So your spirit can't fail to be lifted when you glimpse an envelope with familiar handwriting on it ... it turns out that someone was thinking about you while you were away.

Not long after I first moved to London I went on holiday for two weeks. When I got back my flatmate remarked on how brown I was and asked if I'd been on a sunbed. To add insult to injury, he then refused to believe that I'd been away at all, as he hadn't noticed I'd gone. Making an impact, that's what it's all about ...

This is a lovely message, which would brighten up anyone's day.

I love the spontaneity of text messages, although I'm pretty glad they weren't around when I was young. I would have bombarded the objects of my desire with loving messages. I once discovered that a potential paramour loved the Shamen, so I learned the words to 'Ebenezer Goode' and ensured I was muttering the lyrics whenever I happened to pass him (I can still recite *Boss Drum* if pushed). Pretty embarrassing, of course, but thankfully my shameful secret was only known by a few close, and baffled, friends. I'm almost entirely certain he didn't even notice.

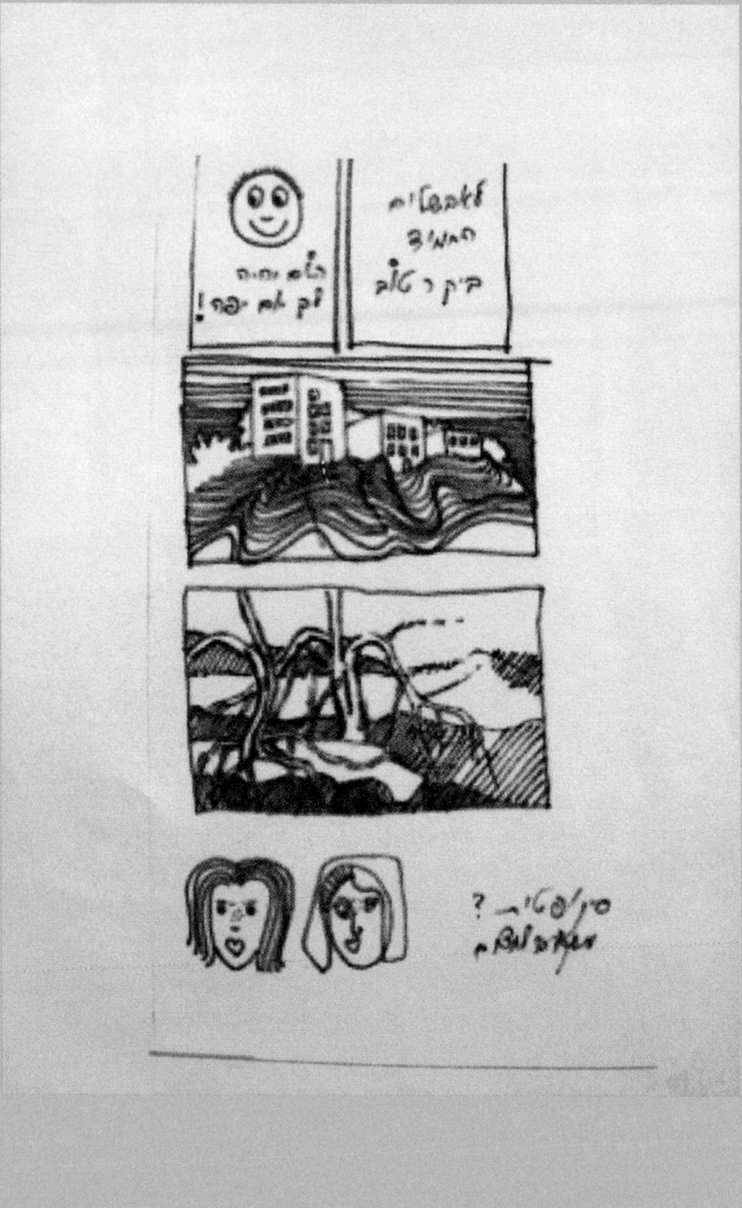

Not all of these notes are about sexual relationships. This one, written in Hebrew (look at us going all international!), is from a mum to her son. I'm told it says, 'Good morning, today you will have a beautiful day.' I think that's lovely. I don't know if you can quantify a mother's love, but the care that has gone into writing this gives some indication of just how much of her heart and mind she's put into bringing up her boy. She apparently left these little inspirational notes for him each morning. Wow … this woman should be a life coach.

I have absolutely no idea if these emails are getting to you but all I really wanted to say was

WAIT

WAIT

WAIT

WAIT

LOVE YOU

Get your FREE download of

This is more like it! This is the kind of mail that everyone likes to see dropping into the inbox. Something that makes all the creepy spam a little less depressing. You know the ones, 'Wait ... wait ... wait ... CHEAP VIAGRA!' Does anyone actually reply to those?

Sometimes it's all about timing. You've woken up with the sort of feeling you get when you're about to sit an exam. That horrible churning in your stomach and an inability to absorb anything that anyone tells you. Then this arrives. A message from a loved one, a fellow space cadet who understands that you have just hit 100 on the panic scale and has made the journey to bring you from Planet Anxiety back down to earth. Suddenly everything feels a little better – just from one little text.

Alrighty Babes,

By the time you've read this, I hope you've had a great weekend, plenty fun, sun, food and intellectual conversation.

WE both know your not going to get any from me, that's intellectual what that is.

I really believe in the ying and the yang. Your time is just around _____. Whether _____

happens _____

Sorry that I can't do any more. I just want to jump on to plane, fly over engulf you in my arms and protect you from all those capitalist corporate money jockeys. We both know you're worth a million of them.

Fuck capitalism who wants to be the same as the next person. Your special and different in your own way stand tall and proud take off those tacky glasses (sorry) hold your head up high, let the see ...

... let the world see that you are twice as bright and infinitely more colourful than your HAIR.

I'm sorry this one's short that problem I have with getting up in the morning. Good luck in selling your soul. If any of those corporate big wigs are worth half the money they paid they they realise your priceless.

I'll be in contact soon, thinking of you always, love and kisses.

This is a fantastic note from a true partner, friend or lover – the sort who'd fight your corner all the way. They see the good in everything you do, and would defend you to the end. Yeah, fuck your boss! Fuck the 'money jockeys'! In fact, in their determination to defend you to the end, they'll even come up with amazing new terminology …

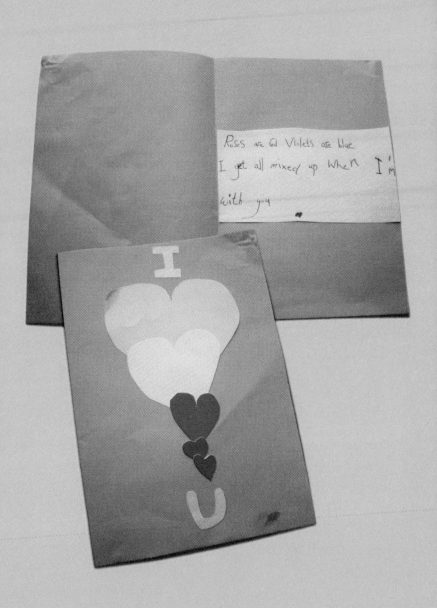

Roses are red Violets are blue
I get all mixed up when I'm
with you

This is a truly touching story. You might look at the scrawl on this message and assume a mentalist penned it, but you would be wrong. The author, a nine-year-old boy whom we'll call Billy, couldn't think of a way to give his valentine a card without alerting his fellow pupils. Think about it – at the age of nine the concept of first class post is a bit alien, and asking someone else to give it to her could lead to a lifetime of bullying.

You know those late night revellers who think they can get their photo taken by a speed camera if they run fast enough? Well, Billy's mind worked in a similar way. At lunchtime, he'd run very, very fast past his beloved's dining table and drop the card in front of her before she could see who had delivered it.

Unfortunately, Billy was only a small boy whose agility was hindered by short legs and puppy fat. He was never going to pick up enough speed to perform his heroic run and drop. So instead of the cartoon-like blur he'd been intending, his valentine saw a small, sweaty boy running towards her, followed by something being thrown at her face. Everyone saw, and everyone laughed. But once she'd stopped crying, Billy's valentine decided the gesture was nice, and that Billy was, well, nice as well … just not a very fast runner.

This part of the letter is

Hiya!

were a bit of a

was telling me on the phone that on holiday you

can read it too

snog donor

to all those lovely

Oh for the days when the sauciest phrase in a teen mag was 'snog donor'. Nowadays you're more likely to encounter the Kama Sutra, with pictures. Back then, snogging was innocent fun, and far less likely to end up in full sex. Your teen years were the last opportunity to indulge in a high turnover of random snogs, so you invariably did. (Donor seems an appropriate word, too, as you probably did a spotty youth or two a favour in the process ...)

I like the word 'snogging' – it's very onomatopoeic, like snuffling, or hugging, or something a piglet would do when out hunting truffles. I guess that's why you do less snogging and more kissing as you get older. Descending on someone as though you're looking for something in the back of their head isn't a technique you want to be using in an adult relationship.

I'm missing you this much →⊔←× *unfortunately*. So *please, please*, keep in touch as much as possible. I love you *zillions* & MAY THE FORCE BE WITH YOU !! ☺ ˙˙ :/ ...they came round this 🙂

Apparently the young man who wrote this letter signed off every note he wrote to his long-distance girlfriend in the same way. For ages she didn't know what he was on about and was especially confused by the crap doodle next to it; whether it was an elaborate signature he had developed, or possibly a monogram of their initials, she just couldn't work it out. When she eventually asked him about it, he was deeply disappointed to find out his girlfriend was not a *Star Wars* fan. Astonishingly, the crappy circle/squiggle turned out to be the logo of the Millennium Falcon. She said she'd try to make it up to him, even wearing her hair in Princess Leia buns, but it was too late; they weren't meant to be. And all because the Millennium Falcon had gone over her head. So to speak.

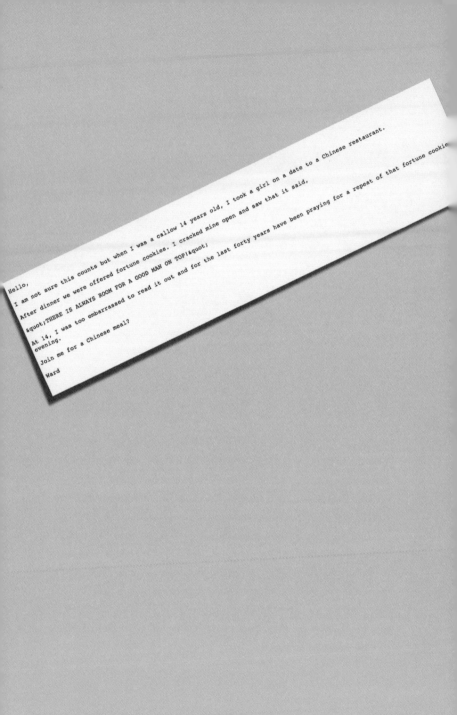

Hello,

I am not sure this counts but when I was a callow 14 years old, I took a girl on a date to a Chinese restaurant.

After dinner we were offered fortune cookies. I cracked mine open and saw that it said,

"THERE IS ALWAYS ROOM FOR A GOOD MAN ON TOP!"

At 14, I was too embarrassed to read it out and for the last forty years have been praying for a repeat of that fortune cookie evening.

Join me for a Chinese meal?

Ward

No bloody wonder the gentleman who sent this note said he was too embarrassed to read his fortune out … they might as well have written 'You deserve a shag' and be done with it!

Even the *concept* of dating is a potential minefield. Take for example the guy at a wedding who, upon being told by a couple at his table that they had only recently started 'dating', asked his fellow diners (none of whom he knew) whether a 'date' was: 1) occasionally meeting up for a coffee; 2) going out for dinner with 'no afters' or 3) going out for dinner, getting schwallied before the starters, skipping the food and heading straight home for 'vaguely satisfying intercourse'.

That's nice to wake up to, isn't it? A little love note, stuck to the bathroom wall. I like the idea of being given helpful instructions like this in the morning. Perhaps the idea could be extended to the elderly, although it might be more appropriate to remind them of their name and location rather than suggesting they indulge in booty shaking.

I'm a little concerned, however, that love notes in the bathroom could easily turn nasty. An argument could result in this becoming 'Shake your BIG FAT booty'. Or worse, 'Why don't you just DROWN YOURSELF?!'

If you're feeling even more creative, these days you can buy pens for writing on bathroom tiles, although in the wrong (young) hands they too could be dangerous. I remember as a child deciding to draw a beautiful big picture of a lovely garden for my mother, on the beautiful big canvas that was our bedroom wall. I can understand why she wasn't exactly overwhelmed. Have you ever tried to paint over oil-based crayons with water-based paint? Not easy.

Come to think of it, the whole idea of leaving messages in the bathroom is a bit fraught; take your mind off the job in hand (getting out of the bath, for instance), and you could come a cropper. So, no to foam letters! No to shaking booties in bathrooms! It's utter madness, and an accident waiting to happen.

CREATIVE LOVE

Oh yeah, you're getting into the swing of this love thing now,
aren't you? This is the fancy pants section, where the creative juices
start flowing and the results look like an episode of *Blue Peter*.
Just mind where you leave that sticky backed plastic ...

Dedicating a song to someone can be very romantic. Not in my case.

I thought he was the best thing since sliced bread. He was funny (sometimes). He was oh so handsome (ok, he was all right looking). I now know he was just a hormonal teenager who fancied himself as a bit of a Casanova. But he liked me (for about a month) and that made me feel brand new. He could have committed every one of the seven deadly sins and I would have let them slip, 'cause he had eyes that made me go a bit weird when he shot me a look. Then something happened. During one hot and steamy afternoon, he stopped mid clinch. 'Wait! Let me play you a song that reminds me of you.' Oh, yes! What could it be? What sensual, sordid song had made him think of me? Which lyric touched his heart so deeply that whenever it was played my smouldering looks would instantly be conjured up?

That would be 'Cuddly Toy', by Roachford.

I don't want to discuss it further, but the hot fires of passion quickly turned to embers. Cuddly? I'm not his bloody granny.

The modern equivalent would be going round to your date's house for the first time and browsing their playlist, only to find S Club 7's Greatest Hits. There's no way of explaining that – just get your coat and run.

Pause, record, stop, rewind, bugger. That was pretty much all I did when I was a kid, listening to the radio trying to record tracks on to cassettes. Those were the days when hearing a whole song was a rarity. With this level of commitment required, it's no wonder 'making a tape' was the ultimate love token. God knows how many hours were spent poring over which songs to choose. How about a bit of Sade, going 'coast to coast, LA to Chicago' to find her Smooth Operator? I never really understood what a smooth operator was. I don't think I've met one to this day, in fact. Or perhaps I have, and it's just that I've always called them wankers.

This picture is particularly good as the compiler-in-chief has taken the time to categorise the tunes, either to suit the mood they are in, or perhaps to bring on the mood they want to be in. Judging by the spelling of the word happiness, this person was pretty depressed at the time!

Shut up, shut up, shut up, shut up.
I love laws. I like knowing all
the answers. I'm great. They all think
I'm great. That's great. This is really
interesting. Gosh, I am interesting.
My voice sounds pretty through this
microphone. I should get one of these
for my house. I could just talk into it and
it would make the goldfish sleepy.
The goldfish loves my voice. I know he
does because when I talk he swims faster.
If there's something charming something
which is a true even... well, hang on
that blonde in the second row

This note is just weird. Totally, utterly weird. Sadly I don't know where it comes from, or for that matter where it was going! It does bring up the topic of loving something else in the absence of a person – perhaps it's a job, or maybe a hobby. You know, the ones who work every hour God sends just so they don't have to think about the fact that when they aren't at work, they have sod all else to do. The ones who will create a spreadsheet at home just to fill in a blank on their 'To Do' list. Then you get the person that realises they have nothing to do outside of work, so they throw themselves into some newly discovered activity. Often these have the ominous title of 'extreme sports'. Why is it that more often than not, these people seem to be extreme dorks? Their obsession with the minutiae of, say, rock climbing (exactly how best to clasp the rope to the wall) would bore any sane person to tears.

Every item in this meal is in the shape of a heart. You may think this is unremarkable, but seeing as I was told that a bloke created it, I think it's pretty cool. This dude would make a killing as a wedding planner.

Erm, thank you? The recipient of this note can't remember what they were being thanked for – not for being a great girlfriend, apparently. The picture was posted to them and they thought it was a bit, well, odd. Mainly because the guy who sent it didn't own a dog. Did he find the dog? Did he think it was from his girlfriend and take the picture to thank her for such a thoughtful present? Maybe he thought it would be nice to send a picture of himself, but worried that it might be a bit dull unless he added a little something else to the scene (a valid, and surprisingly humble, concern)? Or – and hopefully this is not the case – could he have been unaware of the joys of Polaroid photography until now, and in a flush of excitement taken a picture of the first thing that came to hand? Wow, technology! I don't have to send the film to Snappy Snaps!

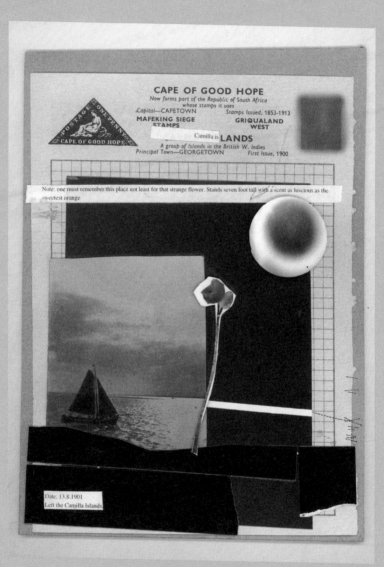

CAPE OF GOOD HOPE

Now forms part of the Republic of South Africa
whose stamps it uses

Capital—CAPETOWN   Stamps Issued, 1853-1913

MAFEKING SIEGE   GRIQUALAND
STAMPS   WEST

Camilla is LANDS

A group of Islands in the British W. Indies
Principal Town—GEORGETOWN   First Issue, 1900

POSTAGE ONE PENNY
CAPE OF GOOD HOPE

Note: one must remember this place not least for that strange flower. Stands seven foot tall with a scent as luscious as the sweetest orange

Date: 13.8.1901
Left the Camilla Islands.

Who said no man is an island? Apparently Camilla is, and she's a lovely one at that. Camilla Island is unique, not least because of its seven-foot, lusciously scented flowers. What a lovely thought, and what a beautiful description. But it could easily have gone so horribly wrong. Imagine an island of small, round, hairy coconuts. Not quite so idyllic.

IMPORTANT!
Is my toothbrush in your room? Please leave by my door
If not, AARGH!
xxxx

Do I detect the undercurrent of a secret tooth brushing fetish here? I don't know about you, but I can't say I love it when someone else cleans my teeth. Let's just imagine for a moment that it *was* an accident. Housemate picks up wrong toothbrush (and fails to notice handy colour coding), saunters into bedroom mid-brush, doesn't bother rinsing, and leaves it there? It doesn't wash with me. I reckon these two are secretly having a relationship and they get their kicks by brushing each other's teeth mid foreplay. Seriously, that's the only sensible answer.

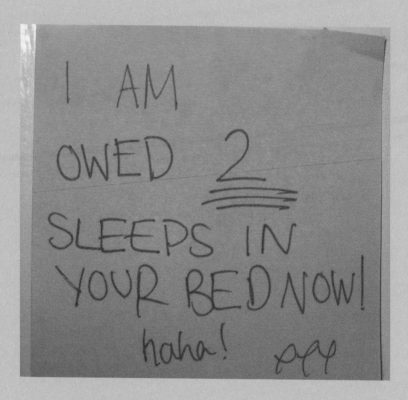

Oh yeah? Little bit brazen this one – it takes the idea of calling in favours to a whole new level if your flatmate's bartering with their morals while the best you can offer is a couple of slices of pizza. I'd love to see what else is on their brothel-like menu. A sleep and a grope (cost: half a pork pie and a Babybel)? Not sure what I would do for two sleeps ...

I think I know what this popcorn party pants message is all about. A friend's cinema date with her boyfriend nearly ended with a slap in the face when she realised that the popcorn box had been fiddled with, and that the contents were more hotdog than popcorn.

Equally disconcerting is the thought that the writer of this is so uncoordinated in the dark. If they can't even get popcorn into their mouth when the lights are out, I'd give them a wide berth ...

The List (In chronological order)

London 2002...
Grand Central
53 Amwell Street
Architect Party
Filthy MacNasty
52 Conduit Street
Soho House
Issey Miyake
Prince Charles Cinema
Tate Modern
Brighton
Secret Rendezvous
Rosemary House
The Rosemary Branch
169 Stroud Green Road
Red Carpet Nights
Devon camping
Ballina, Ireland
Crockets On The Quay
Barcelona
Valparaiso
Chiloe
Surprise parties
6 Coleridge Court

to be continued... ♡

I liked Tracey Emin's tent scrawled with the names of all the people she had slept with, but would be far too timid to do it myself. This, on the other hand, is a beautiful idea. A secret list, containing names of significance only to the couple in question. Fortunately 'round the back of the bike sheds' or 'the number 38 to Hackney' don't appear – otherwise something very charming could become quite terrifying.

Centenary Beauty
10 University Square,
Glasgow,
G12 8QQ.

Tel: (0141) 330 5897
Fax: (0141) 330 5566
e-mail: beauty@gla.ac.uk

UNIVERSITY
of
GLASGOW

Dear Mr. ████

It is with great pleasure that I write to you and invite you to the first sessions of interviews for Glasgow University's *Centenary Beauty*. After long hours looking through the many matriculation pictures that all Glasgow students have to have taken we stumbled across a picture of you. We believe that you could be the face of Glasgow University for the next century.

The Centenary Beauty winner will have their picture taken and passed all around the world in our *International Press Pack*, with possible visits to Tasmania, Poland and the Outer Hebrides. You will also have to be host for many of the receptions that Glasgow University holds through out the year. And finally, perhaps most importantly, your bust will be sculptured from granite and displayed in the new *Centenary Monument*, placed just infront of the flag poles on the North side of campus.

If you are interested in taking part then please phone me directly on 0141-330-5360 extension 28, just to tell me when we can meet and get this interview over with. You could be Glasgow of the future!

Yours sincerely,

M.████

Michael ████
Head of Centenary Celebration.

You've got to admit this is a smart move – I'd fall for it hook, line and sinker. The big plan, of course, is to get your hands on your college paramour's bust, and what better way to do this than to send her a letter telling her she's a shoe-in for the university's Centenary Beauty pageant? OK, so perhaps this is on the slimy side of smart, but I'd date him just to reward him for the time taken to fit all the crests, fonts and other stuff together – true dedication to the Centenary cause.

This is
page 7
Number
33
Physique
Pictorial

Lipstick on your what? Eeeeuw, that's a bit gross. At least it makes it clear what you think, feel and might do ...

← it is his sting not something else

← fur

Mr. Furry Bee has a wry smile. He is a symbol of excitement, sensuality and sexuality. MR. FURRY BEE KNOWS EVERYTHING — he is so small he can bee anywhere at anytime. We WORSHIP the phallic shaped furry bees.
* BREATHLESSNESS
* EROTICISM
* EXCITEMENT

Only those who understand Mr. Furry Bee can worship him. You are one of those people. He chooses his worshippers very carefully hence when he flew round your legs today. Always bee on the lookout and always think of what Mr. Furry Bee stands for. He lives in the HIVE which is why we are always drawn to the buzzing night life there.

from a MR. FURRY. BEE worshipper.

phallic shaped bee hive

62

Acronyms are very useful when it comes to love. Until surprisingly recently, posh young ladies would become debutantes in order to meet similarly posh young chaps. As they weren't allowed to openly discuss their feelings, they developed acronyms to let their mates know exactly what was on their minds. So for instance, MTF stood for Must Touch Flesh (when dancing, I presume, as anything else would've been scandalous). Anyway, codes like this have stuck around, even if the idea of a debut hasn't. So here we have the BEE of Breathless Erotic Excitement, complete with a handy logo. My only concern is that there are a few references to the phallic shape of the bee, which is surely stretching the idea a little too far (unless the gentlemen they've been dating are, er, unusually shaped). I'd be looking for Sexy New Adventurous Kinky Excitement instead, thank you very much.

hope you have the best birthday (you should
do as I'm in your life haha!) but seriously
hope you have a tremendous day and get
everything you asked for, you deserve nothing less
HAPPY BIRTHDAY! 😊 ← how you make
                          me feel.

I love you so much and   (happy, if you were
I don't know what I'd do   thinking a big round
              without you,   head with no body)

x x x x x x x
x x x x x x x

Ah, the ubiquitous smiley face. Long gone are the days when a smiley face was synonymous with raves in muddy fields and taking acid. This scribe feels a natural high brought on by love. Alas, it hasn't quite removed their very British sense of propriety, as they've still felt compelled to clear up any confusion.

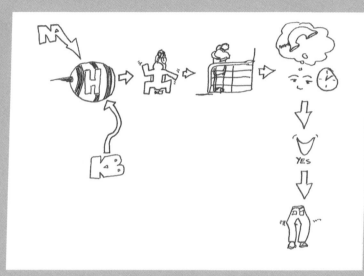

This is a sort of visual representation of a first date ... it obviously left him speechless!

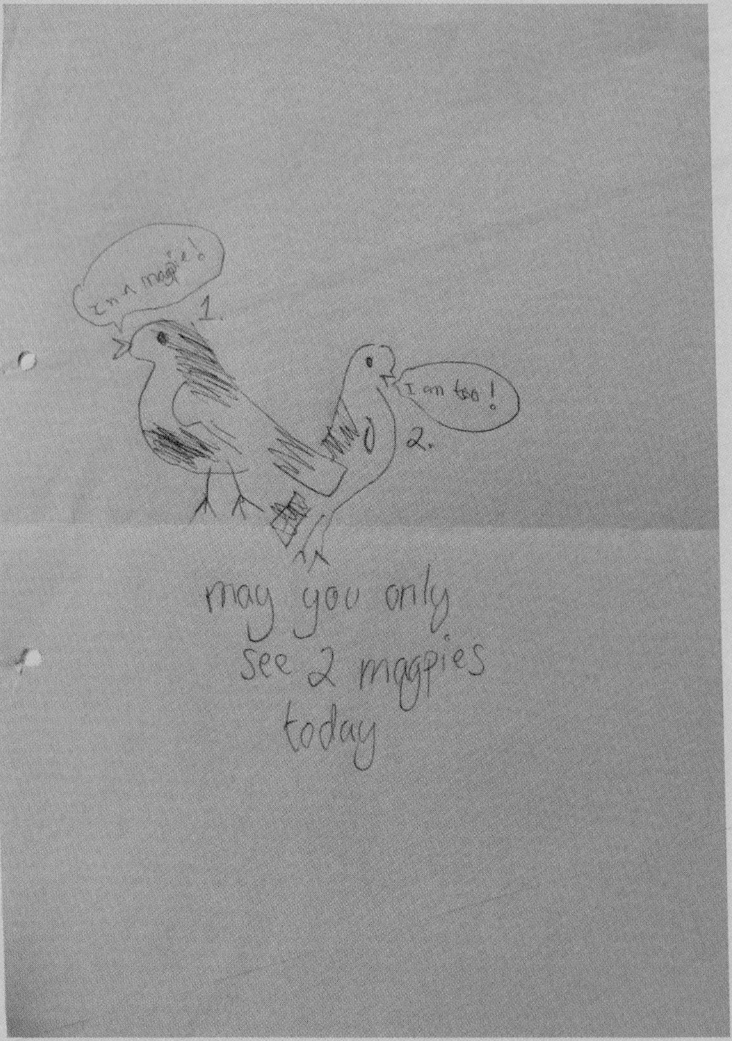
I'm a magpie!
1.
I am too!
2.
may you only
see 2 magpies
today

This is a very sweet way of wishing your beloved a day filled with joy. You know the rhyme, *One for sorrow, two for joy, three for a girl, four for a boy*? All because magpies stick with their mate, so if you see one on its own there's probably a sad story in there somewhere. I still salute if I see a magpie. Or in this instance, a mangy pigeon-like thing ...

I'm all for handmade gifts. It's a sign of a good relationship when someone is prepared to have a go at stuff (perhaps they'll turn out to be good at DIY too?). It's all too easy these days to buy something from the internet with a few clicks of the mouse, or to pick up a cheap bunch of flowers from the supermarket. Taking the time to make a present is much more thoughtful. Then again I would say that – I once made a boyfriend a gigantic Jaffa Cake, a favourite of his. Even if the gift ends up being crap (which my Jaffa Cake most certainly wasn't), or you're not the creative type, it doesn't matter. You never know, you might quite enjoy doing it, and the idea might take off in any number of ways. Just recently I found a whole website dedicated to my gift idea (www.pimpthatsnack.com), and I wouldn't be surprised if even the humble paperclip started as a budget pressie to a loved one.

Ah, the domestic bliss of the long-term relationship. Apparently the boyfriend who did this had been promising to fix the washing machine for ages and on realising that yet another weekend was about to pass without him doing it, he turned it into a vase. With that sweet thought he probably got himself out of jail for the time being, but I bet he'll get it sorted when he runs out of underpants.

EUPHORIC LOVE

This is the 'I don't give a damn if you think I'm a tosser, I'm in love!' section. Professional lovers know to avoid this area – it's pretty hazardous …

This person is pumped and ready for action – I'd take cover if I were you. I don't know the circumstances of its creation, but I'd guess this note was written after a particularly heavy night out – the sort of situation where anything seems possible but lovin' isn't always likely.

It's no secret that when under the influence, you often feel able to take on the world. A little investigation revealed a few more unusual examples of alcohol-induced projects that friends of mine have taken on, such as: engraving every glass bottle in the house with own name, trying to dance with a budgie (and nearly causing its premature death), eating three kebabs in quick succession, and failing to put shoes on before going out.

Big talk, and big ideas, should be a big no-no after a few bevies. Drink may make the mind say yes, but generally this is shortly followed by the body passing out. And with this in mind, my guess is that the Beastoramic was more of a Disappointoramic.

A note from

You complete me.
I love you.
I'm sorry that
it has come
to this.
Goodbye.

Call me cold-hearted or a cynic, but this note makes me want to vomit. I also think it is such a huge thing to say to someone that you shouldn't write it down ... especially not in this very girly handwriting. And check out the notepaper ... don't people grow out of buying this kind of stationery when they hit puberty?

To say that someone completes you, to imply that they are the missing piece to the enigma that is life, is a big old weight to put on that person's shoulders. You'd have to be mighty sure that they aren't going to run a frigging mile when they read it. Of course it also suggests that the author has something missing – I suspect in this case it's their marbles. Poor thing – I can't help thinking that after sending this message they're going to remain, well, incomplete.

I AM SO HAPPY AND GRATEFUL
NOW I HAVE:

. A WORLD - CLASS MANAGER + 'DEAL'
- £3 million (_____)
. CRITICAL INDUSTRY BUZZ

If you were with this person, and you came across this note, you could be forgiven for struggling to maintain an objective opinion about them and their £3 million (who cares about the 'critical industry buzz' eh?). It reminds me of the brilliant Mrs Merton interview with Debbie McGee, where she asked, 'So what was it that first attracted you to the millionaire Paul Daniels?'

This person's feel good list puts mine to shame. It reads:
* Sorted emails into appropriate files
* Cut down on swearing
… end of list.

As long as I know you want to give this a try then I'm willing with all my heart to prove to you there is NO ONE else. (- How terribly "soppy" I have become!)

Amidst all This I'll admit realizing that subconsciously I have failed to mention what I most mean to tell you by using such words as "feelings" and "views" - no where do I mention love (perhaps through fear of scaring you off).

I love you

This is a lovely but difficult letter to write. The sort that gets written when you become aware that you've told someone they're smashing, cool, amazing, major ... but have managed to avoid actually saying you love them. So here it is in black and white.

Cor blimey, missus. This note made me go all weak at the knees ...
and it wasn't even meant for me! That in itself can be a problem –
I think at some stage in our lives we've all sent a text to the wrong
person. The one sent to a friend instead of your other half asking her
what she wants to do tonight is bearable. The one telling them you
want to see them naked when they get home from work is best just
flatly denied, in my opinion. Trying to explain to the confused friend
that the lusty message was for someone else is just humiliating: 'No,
no, I didn't want to see *you* naked, not that I don't think you would
look great naked, oh God ...'

The joy of text is that it's quick and it's immediate. Just like the sassy
thought that pops into your head when you're least expecting it, texts
often arrive unannounced. There's nothing more exciting than the
sensation in your trousers that accompanies the arrival of a message
from a new love. There's nothing *less* exciting than finding the vibration
has been caused by your phone provider asking if you want a new
bundle of something or other. Although there's bound to be someone
out there who finds that sort of thing erotic, of course.

We are, are we? Gosh, talk about bravado. Actually, this has definitely been written after a few drinks. Who cares? It's a cool message ... 'Us against the world'.

This relationship is obviously a team effort in which neither party has let the side down. I suppose thinking of a relationship in terms of it being a team is quite good – you'd have to think about roles, skills, strengths, weaknesses, maybe uniforms ...

What is it about uniforms that people think is saucy? And why is it always nurses or firemen? Perhaps it's got something to do with people in authority, in which case why don't people in Superdrug or Currys get a look in? I'm quite partial to the odd name badge and a polyester sweater.

I MISS U
EVERY MINUTE
WE'RE APART AND
SEPARATE,
I LONG FOR US
TO MAKE IT LAST
LONG AND GREAT!

XXXXXO

Very determined, this one. Looks like something Churchill might have written. It almost feels as though the couple are entering a battle they may never come back from. That's one way of looking at a relationship, I suppose.

The First Flush

You're up and running! Love is in the air, you feel happy, sick and giddy all at once, and want to spin round trees in parks, smile at strangers and burst into spontaneous song … this is no longer a potential love situation, it's the real thing. You're in the honeymoon period, that knee-trembling phase in a relationship when the apple of your eye can do no wrong, also known as the time when you lose all sense of reality, dignity and sanity. Your brain turns to the consistency of a sticky toffee pudding and your stomach feels as warm as if you've just had a big portion of one. Talking of big portions, this is when you will be getting physical – it's all new, exciting and unexplored territory and takes up 99 per cent of your time. You couldn't give a toss that you're talking about it 24/7 and that you're now doing all the cheesy/romantic things that are part and parcel of the happy world of wooing and dating. (You know, all the things that you normally sneer at when you're in your single state.)

In most cases, these heady days are when the majority of love notes are penned. Declarations about infinite amounts of time and never ending levels of love are tossed around. Thousands of text messages are sent every day, each one containing so many kisses you end up with RSI in your thumbs. You're constantly talking in superlatives.

This is a time that your colleagues and boss dread. Your boss hates it because your mind is on another sort of job. Your work colleagues hate it because you become a relationship bore, or worse still, a relationship boaster. You start telling anyone who'll listen how 'you just knew' it was love at first sight (the pivotal role that alcohol played has been conveniently airbrushed from the picture). Nonetheless, deep down most people are rooting for you, and hoping that this really is 'the one' – especially as you have just made a prat of yourself talking about your amazing intuition.

But who cares what everyone else thinks anyway? This chapter is the 'Once upon a time' bit of the fairytale, where all your hard work is beginning to pay off. You're full of bravado and rightly so. Enjoy it. Feel happy ... smug even. Be condescending to singletons and be sure to give them plenty of top tips to improve their own sad lives.

SAUCY/FETISH LOVE

Hmmm. Crack open the chocolate body paint and get the thumbscrews on. Hold on to the bedpost, we're going in, and it's going to be Filthy McNasty. This section's going to make your eyes water ... it's the saucy bit, you hussies!

Call me crazy but I'm just not that into noses. I remember learning about how sensitive they are in a Biology lesson. We were instructed to test this by rubbing our own snouts over various different metals and identifying which were the thickest. Or perhaps the teacher was taking the piss.

If it is such a sensitive protrusion, then I guess it makes sense that it could be an erogenous zone, but I'm not convinced. Sure, it's interesting to come across a Cyrano de Bergerac or a Pinocchio, but more in a 'that's a helluva beak' than a 'that's so erotic I simply have to have a suck on it' kind of way. No, I'm definitely not into draining the dregs of a cold out of somebody's conk. Although I am intrigued about how far people take the fetish. Can you get tiny, studded PVC harnesses to wear on your nose as you get it whipped?

I can see why this is a note – it's always mortifying to discover housemates in compromising positions, but this one has to be the weirdest yet. In fact, I'm tempted to create an award for the most unusual sexual request. Breadcrumbs in a belly button? Large weights being hung off earlobes while having chin licked? So much to try, so little time!

I like big butts and I cannot lie, you other brothers can't deny ... oh sorry, I slipped into the persona of 'Sir Mix-a-Lot' there ... hey, maybe Sir Mix-a-Lot sent me this note? Are these the first scribbles of his illustrious career? Have I uncovered the original lyrics for 'Baby Got Back'? Don't they auction this kind of stuff? John Lennon's lyrics for 'Imagine' went for thousands of dollars. This could be my nest egg. If you don't know what I am talking about, have a listen on t'internet and shake your big butt! In fact, the more people you get to do this, the more likely I am to clean up in the auction. In the meantime, I want to know if it is true? Are big butts a plus and not just a plus size? Personally I think it comes down to shape and texture. A rectangular doughy bottom is not as attractive as a peach of an arse. Yes, this is where we get to the bottom of the big butt debate. Alliteration and a pun; I have hit a comedy low.

I can't tell if this is a nice note ('I'm extending my fruits to you as a show of generosity') or a nasty one ('Fuck you, shove my fruits up your arse' sort of thing).

I'd be a little wary of eating someone else's fruit, particularly something as phallic as a banana. I once knew a rather prudish young lady who refused to eat them in public as she was worried it might look like fellatio, the dirty minx. Why is it that straight-laced people are often verging on pervy? I blame the Victorians (again!), obsessed as they were with covering everything up with their oppressive clothing, and bursting at the seams to get their leg over as a result.

As for me, I'm worried that writing this book has turned me into a sex-crazed maniac who finds innuendo and filth in everything. Just don't get me started on cucumbers and plums – the work of the devil!

"As the train gently rumbles along... I picture you relaxing on a giant milky way chocolate bar floating through space. Your coffee coloured skin bathed in nothing but delicate shimmering moonlight. The stars are gently flickering in a vain attempt to compete, but their light looks pale against the delicious contours of your heavenly form. How I long to visit you in my dairy milk moonship.xxxps. its snowingxxxx"

This is a prime example of what happens when love makes you all dazed and confused (and when you spend long enough on a train journey for your thoughts to stray into fantasy).

This message – a text – is like a scene from *Easy Rider*, it's verging on the trippy and sounds quite fun. There's something about a written message that makes it easier to say things than face to face. In this instance if the author had told his girlfriend he wanted to visit her in his Dairy Milk moon ship, I reckon he'd have got a slap (or sectioned!).

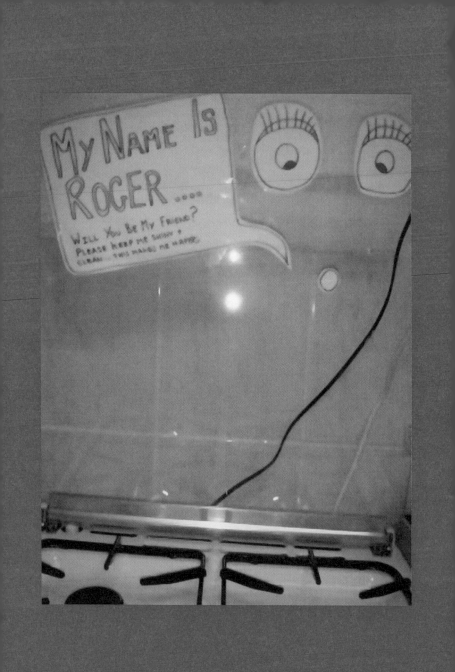

Is it me, or is someone trying to suggest that inanimate objects need love too? Come on now, don't be shy – haven't you ever thought about thrusting against your washing machine, or making love to your car? Oh, you have ...? What the hell's wrong with you? Sicko.

Yes, I detect the hand of a mechaphile (someone who's sexually attracted to machines) in this note. You start by simply cleaning Roger's hot rings and oiling his door and before you know it you find yourself loving his hood and wanting to be a lot more than just friends. And there I was thinking sexual attraction to machinery was limited to certain battery operated devices that you can pick up in Soho, the ones with names like 'bunny popper'. Haven't we run out of things to get off on yet?

Don't you get it? Roger doesn't want to be loved. He wants to be left alone, or at most to be able to cook a nice Sunday roast for you. He is an oven, he doesn't love you. Get over it. And stop making eyes at the microwave.

What the hell have you been wearing if you end up having to put this sign up on your front door? There's dressing to impress, and then there's dressing like a lady of the night.

I can sympathise with this one actually. In my flat sharing days I lived in a place with five rooms. A few times I answered the door late at night, only to be confronted by shifty men asking for girls with names like Candy and looking distinctly disappointed at the sight of me in my baggy t-shirt and tracksuit bottoms. It was only after this had happened five or six times that I twigged that the flat had been a brothel in a previous life. Now I come to think of it, maybe the huge locks on the internal doors were a bit of a hint.

If a big, black, rubber cock shaped parcel arrives ____ could you put it in the bread bin?

Ah, how times have changed in the world of porn. Gone is the furtive side-step into a 'special shop', exiting moments later clutching a brown paper bag hiding your magazine of choice. With the arrival of the internet and its plethora of websites to suit all tastes, everyone can indulge their own peculiar sexual preference.

Not only that, but it seems that now this sort of stuff is so easily available we've forgotten our sense of decorum. What ever happened to the days when even mentioning the word 'cock' would have caused gasps of disapproval? Nowadays it seems you can scrawl it on a note, or even chuck it in a breadbin … Oh for the good old days of 'top shelf innocence'.

You might be mistaken for thinking that this is a cry for help from a serial killer (after all, everyone needs to be loved). But no, it's an appeal from a poorly lady. You can test the depths of your partner's love by figuring out how far they're willing to go when you're unwell. If they mop your brow and hold your hair back while you're puking in the toilet, that's love. If they don't flinch when you break off a passionate embrace to make a mad dash for the loo when you've got a dodgy tummy, then you know they're the one. And if they find you attractive when you're beached on the sofa with snotty tissues piling up around you, that's it – you've got a keeper!

It's interesting to see certain topics cropping up more than once in this book. How the Victorians have totally fucked up how we think about love and sex, for instance.

This brooch illustrates another of their fascinations – death. Well, love, death and fashion to be more precise. In Victorian times, the fashionable thing to do following the death of a loved one was to turn their hair into a bracelet, or teeth into jewellery. I've actually got a hairy bracelet, but can't bring myself to touch it.

Actually, this particular brooch was meant to be a love token, believe it or not. It is a child's baby teeth and intended to be a gift for the mother. I'm not big on biological love tokens to be honest. Angelina Jolie famously wore a vial of Billy Bob Thornton's blood around her neck when she was married to him. And to trump that, a lady called Joni Mabe owns a preserved wart that was removed from Elvis Presley's hand. Shame the King didn't sing the immortal line, 'Every time you go away, you take a piece of me with you ...'

Can any members of the household lucky enough to be enjoying a sexual relationship please save your, erm, prophylactic wrappings ... I want to make a dress with them.

Thank you, and enjoy yourselves.

:)

Sagely !

You know you've hit a sexual low (as opposed to your libido, which has clearly hit a high) when you start basing art projects around other people's used condoms.

Mind you, the artiste will probably make millions and we will see said skirt in the museum of modern art next year. Why have I spent my life collecting notes when Durex could've made me so much richer? Silly me.

After catching
You sniffing
my girlfriends
tights – taken
from laundry
basket in
MY room
(You disgusting
wanker)
please get
out of
my house
by 9am
Sunday – please
just FUCK OFF

108

'Catching' and 'sniffing' are two words you really don't want to see in a sentence about a girlfriend's tights. I wish they had said more about what region was being sniffed though. The crotch? The feet? Or the whole length of the leg, like a fine Cuban cigar? I can see why the author is so annoyed – they'll never be able to look at the perpetrator again without thinking of the heinous crime.

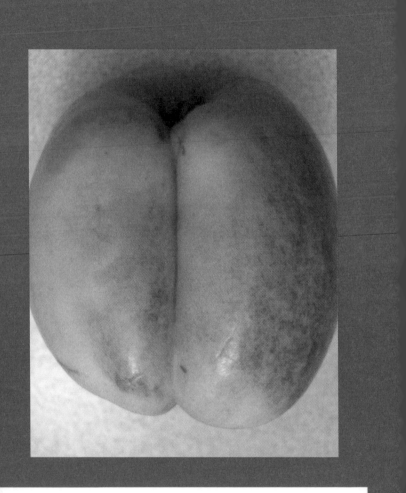

I think I can see why Adam found Eve's apple so tempting now.

It's a shame we can't see where this picture was taken. It would be a bit off-putting if it was the centrepiece of a table on a romantic date. You couldn't even move it onto someone else's table without looking like you were propositioning them.

LOVE WALK SE5
LONDON BOROUGH OF SOUTHWARK

I think I might have seen a 'love walk' in action when I was at school. My male friends inform me that, for teenage boys, it's not unusual for the old flagpole to go to full mast for no reason at all. It sounds terrifying, like a pubescent version of Tourette's. If there was a bit of my body I couldn't control – my leg, for example – I'd be a gibbering wreck. Just now and again my leg shooting out, tripping up random strangers and making me look, well, weird.

It is not just lust that cranks it up though. Apparently being very nervous or frightened can also cause it to stand to attention; a fact that may explain the incident I'm referring to. I think it was before a maths exam. Having located our seats, we all had to get up and put our coats and bags at the front of the hall so we couldn't get anything out of them and cheat. One unfortunate young man, who was sitting at the back of the hall, only seemed able to use his legs from the knees down. As a result he was shuffling along so slowly that by the time he got to the front, the rest of us had returned to our seats and were just staring at this bizarre behaviour. Once he'd dropped his bag and turned around, it became clear that he'd either become extremely nervous or curiously excited about long division. Poor boy – these things come up at such impractical times.

Love Walk isn't the most amusing London street name I've seen – without a doubt that would have to be Gropecunt Street. Sorry, did that give you a bit of a shock? This evocatively named alley was where prostitutes hung out, and apparently there were 'Gropecunt Streets' across the UK. You may be glad to hear that it no longer exists. It was renamed Milton Street after Gropecunt upset some people's sensibilities. I can't think why.

Silly place names are a source of amusement across the world, of course. I have a great picture of my father in the middle of Intercourse, Pennsylvania. There are two Twatts in Scotland, and it always seems a little ironic there is a Fingringhoe in Essex.

Hi
We get married next week and are they away on honeymoon from 23 July – 4 August. So I don't think that we will need cleaning on 24th or 31st July. Is this ok with you?
Thanks

Hi
CONGRATULATION!
IF YOU NOT NEED I'LL CAME IT'S OK!
BUT HAVE YOU PAY THE SAME USE EVERBODY PAY WHEN

YOU REMEMBER?
THANKS.

I CAN DO CLEAN INSIDE CABBAGE, ORGANIZE CLOTHES.

You're getting married. The venue's booked, the dress has been pressed ... but crumbs, have the cabbages been cleaned? This note is from a cleaner with very good intentions, who presumably is worried about the cupboards being clean when the happy couple return from their honeymoon. Or judging by the slightly broken English, perhaps well-polished cabbages are a traditional love token exchanged by newlyweds in her homeland. Perhaps it's got something to do with a legend about a baby being found in a cabbage patch? Or perhaps not.

I AM SORRY I HAD TO PUT MY PEE IN THE FRIDGE. I SEALED IT IN A PLASTIC BAG, THEN THE BOX, THEN TAPED IT SHUT. ♡ c

You really must love someone if you're cool with them leaving boxes (well, actually, bottles inside bags inside boxes) of pee next to your food. It brings a new meaning to the phrase 'in sickness and in health' when you can begin a conversation with, 'Hey honey, I'm just going to sling your bag of piss into the freezer.' If this had been left unlabelled it could have been mistaken for a particularly acidy apple juice or tangy vinaigrette …

115

"Well I guess" I'll wrap up now. I hope you like my notepaper even though its not as good as the headed paper I sent u 4'.
Lots of Luv '

PS - I'm really into super cars and my favourite is the Ferrari F40. Would please consider being phots'd with one? If you did, I could die with a big smile on my face!!

As Prefab Sprout suggested in their 80s hit, there's more to life than cars and girls ... unless you're the type of person who uses car shaped notepaper, that is. I love themed stationery, but I worry that this looks more like a Citroën Dolly than a Ferrari F40. Mind you, perhaps that's a reflection of the girl he's writing to.

```
Darling        .
        Hi there  darling, it's your      .       .     here.
Many thanks for your  ˜    · ··    ·    .   ·.   ˙       quite
safely.
        I am sitting writing this to you inm my Stockings,
Suspenders,  _          , and Knickers,




 - ----- ----




                With all my LOVE and KISSES



            XXXXXXXXXXXXXXXXXXXXXXXX
```

Talk about brief and to the point! I have a lot of time for people who don't mince their words – us Scots have a reputation for telling it like it is, and I'm glad to see that this man (didn't I mention it was from a bloke to a girl?) is quite happy to let it nearly all hang out while he writes his love letters. I suppose wearing skimpy ladies' knick-knacks gets him into the mood.

118

I can't decide if this has been written by a Somerset farmer or a pirate. 'Ooh arrrr me hearties, I 'as finded your dildos.' It makes me think of poor Long John Silver accidentally boarding a sex holiday cruise where the only gold booty he could find had three speeds and required a couple of double A batteries.

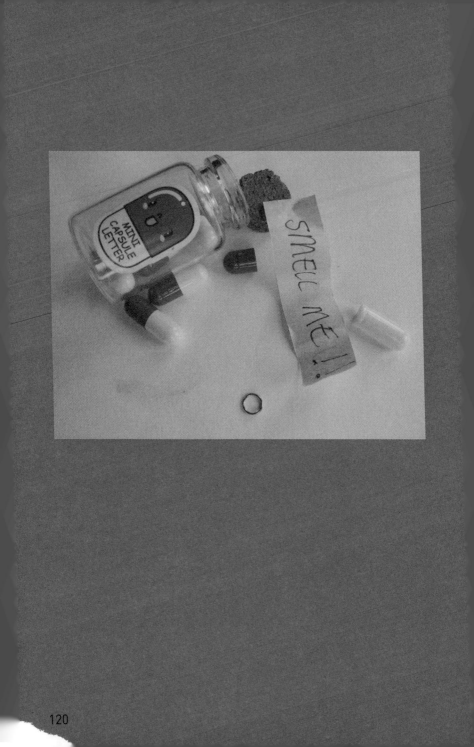

I'm always impressed at the lengths some people will go to demonstrate their love. Writing this book has made me realise that it's not just the notes themselves, but the time and effort that have been put into the gesture that are remarkable. It could be just a few words, but if you know that the author struggles to express their feelings, then it makes the note that bit more special.

This is a story about an asthmatic, Ralph Lauren, and some love potion. The person who contributed this tale told me that it may not have been the most classic of romantic gestures, but it certainly got points for effort. Her boyfriend at the time decided to take the empty Ventolin medicine capsules that he had for his asthma, insert a very small love note into each one, spray it with his aftershave (this is where Ralph comes in), before sealing them all back up. The result was that the young lady could have a 'love pill' every day. When she opened it, not only would it contain a soppy, sorry, *poignant* love message, but it would also smell of her boyfriend! I thought this was amazing, thoughtful, and a bit strange. So it was to my utter astonishment that after hearing the story I found this bottle of 'pills' in a shop importing Japanese stuff. Sure enough, it contains little capsules that you crack open and insert your very own little love notes into! Ventolin guy was a genius – if he could have bottled that idea he would have made a fortune … the Ralph Lauren of love notes!

please
inform me of your
measurements bra
size ie chest measurements
waist measurements
hip measurements
hang think um being rude
I want to buy you a
P.V.C. BIKINI for your
holidays.
LUV love

I like tase yours
lips on face
xx

NEXT TIME

This is a saucy one, but I think the gentleman who wrote it might have misunderstood. It's one thing wearing PVC underwear, if that's what floats your boat, but a PVC bikini? I can't think of anything worse than having to wear this on holiday. Have you ever sat on the plastic seat of a car when it's been baking in the sun? So sweaty and uncomfortable. Never mind that, imagine getting sand in your PVC bikini bottoms, you'd be chafed to death every which way you turned. I just hope the author means underwear, otherwise their night of love is going to involve a lot of camomile lotion.

Having said that, he does say 'your' holiday – is he not going with her? This is pretty weird – maybe he likes the idea of her discomfort. In which case, if I were her, I'd use the bikini as a sling shot if he came within 100 yards.

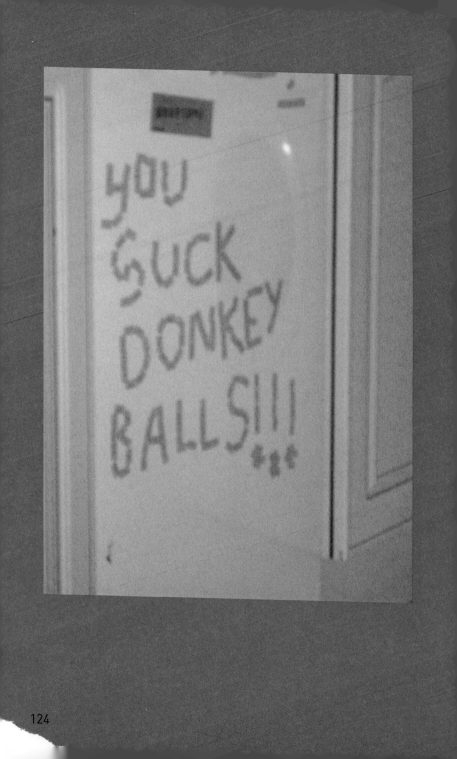

That's not very nice, is it?

This person is obviously hurt and angry with the ball sucker, and the note works well – it's both humiliating and demonstrates the author's rage very effectively. I suppose if you were only a little bit angry and hurt at the person you might accuse them of sucking mice balls, or seahorse balls, or anything else with an extremely small scrotum. Or perhaps instead of sucking it might say, 'you sometimes think about touching donkey balls'. Less in your face, but still quite a putdown.

I don't get all this obsession with sucking anyway. It seems very American. I prefer straightforward comparisons to anatomy: bottoms, penises, etc. Just straightforward nouns and adjectives thank you. But where have the traditional derogatory insults gone? Where's a twat when you need one?

OBSESSIVE LOVE

We were getting along okay with the saucy bit,
but this is the area that turns a bit sick, to be perfectly honest.
This is where your secret admirers turn into your stalkers.
Don't say I didn't warn you ...

20 Dull pain (4)

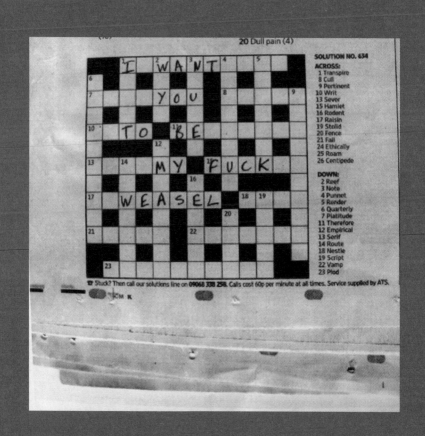

I was disappointed not to be able to track down the author or recipient of this note to ask them the pressing questions that I'm sure you may have, too (not that I spend my time fantasising about animals – let me be totally clear about that). Why a weasel? Surely a stallion would have been a more appropriate animal than this rodent? What would a fuck weasel look like, anyway? It sounds like something out of one of those sci-fi/porno hybrid films where women are bred for all sorts of tasteful purposes. And then thanks to the Urban Dictionary I discovered that 'fuck weasel' is a charming expression defined as, 'a horrible looking girl used primarily for one night stands after a bottle of vodka; she has both fuck and weasel like qualities'. Pretty direct as chat-up lines go, but not terribly romantic ...

Hello,
I am in the class next
door - I have noticed
you - you are very
good lookeny. I have a
crush on you. I wanna have
a drink w me?
notso ♡ secret admirer

xxx

130

You can only hope and pray this is not from a teacher …

This is more of a love portrait than a love note. Initially it seems terribly flattering, but on reflection it's actually a bit frightening. Somebody who studies you from afar and can record and replicate your every detail is either something you find totally irresistible or a tiny teeny weenie bit scary. I think it *could* fall into the category of being a really cool romantic gesture, if the piece of art shows skill and maybe even an uncanny likeness. But when it strays into Lionel Ritchie video territory, that's just plain wrong. Remember the video for 'Hello' where the girl makes a sculpture of Lionel's head and it's, er, rubbish? It looks as though she's taken a shovel to a massive wad of plasticine in order to achieve that fine level of detail. Ok, I understand she's blind, and the whole scenario isn't real, and it is just a music video, but let's face it, Lionel must have been a tiny bit perturbed to see the end result. I'm surprised he didn't protest … 'Guys, could we slightly change the theme of the video? Maybe a quick sketch rather than a shit clay head sculpture-thingy?' How someone else sees you can sometimes destroy a blossoming relationship. You have been warned.

I particularly like this note, as it sums up how easily admiration can turn into obsession. I've often wondered why the most unlikely public figures seem to attract these types. Take newsreaders, for instance – they're always a big hit with the stalking fraternity. Is it something to do with the fact that they're beamed into your home each night? 'Hello Trevor McDonald, fancy seeing you here again! Come on, you obviously want me; you're always in my living room . . . '

The first time I really understood that stalkers weren't just eager fans was when I saw the scene in *The Bodyguard* where Whitney Houston's bed is violated by a masturbating 'fan'. The film was ruined for me after that – not by the act itself, but by Kevin Costner talking about masturbating, which, unless you're a menopausal woman (mums love the Costner, no matter what he's talking about), just seems wrong.

This note shows a worrying level of horror over the death of Frank Butcher, either from a fan of his, or possibly a general *EastEnders* lover. It's a little worrying, and indicative of the stalker mentality, that they don't seem to know the difference between Mike Reid the actor (who had died) and Frank Butcher the character (who was always dead as he was never really alive, if you see what I mean).

PLEASE

What it is to love and yet not to have.
To lie here screaming in my mind.
The thought of you and wind is
So unkind.

At night when winter nights have fallen
And the playful wind rustles the trees.
I think of holding you near me.
Please —

Good grief. You go out for quiet drink, buy a couple of rounds, and the next time you go to the bar you're presented with this by an unhinged barman. Let's be clear, this is not sweet, this is psycho. Did the barman write it there and then, or is he stockpiling these soliloquies behind the bar next to the sliced lemon? He's chancing his arm and his job. I've only had something like this happen to me twice in my life. A barman in Spain once gave me a picture of himself with a kiss on the back. I only asked for a drink and he seemed to think I was giving him the big come on. Maybe he was famous in Spain and was used to handing out pictures of himself? Very weird. The second time was when I had my jacket taken from a nightclub. I left my name and number with the manager in case they found it. He called me the next night, not with my jacket but with a proposal to go on a date. Again, I just wanted my jacket. I couldn't figure out if I had to go on the date to get the jacket. In the end I decided just get a new jacket.

Hey,

Because I don't wear contacts or glasses in the gym, I can only see as far as the dumbells hovering over my nose. But the only other thing I seem to be able to focus on and be distracted by is you, so I was hoping that if you were in a bit of a mischievous and frivolous mood, you would give me a call or text and I would be able to get to know you better. Here's hoping

This is impressive. It seems a young man in a gym took his eye off his pedometer and let his thoughts, and eyes, stray towards a more attractive form of exercise. He left this note on her exercise machine. That takes some bravery, and it was lucky for the bloke that the girl was merely flattered and didn't turn round and smack him in the mouth. Indeed, it was lucky that she was the one who picked up the note … imagine if someone else had queue jumped. Awkward.

Although this didn't develop into a long-term relationship, the pair did go on some dates, so well done to them both. Getting asked out in a gym wouldn't really be my cup of tea, to be honest, although I doubt it would ever happen given that I'm not one of these Lycra clad gym bunnies that kiss their guns in the mirrors every ten seconds. I find mirrors depressing in a gym. Seeing myself struggling to breathe every which way I look doesn't encourage me to keep going – it just makes me want to cry over a piece of cake.

I *have* been involved in a blossoming romance at a swimming pool, mind you. I was busy trying to make my last length and as I stretched out to touch the side I popped up between a couple looking longingly into each other's eyes. Flirting in a pool seems a little uncouth – had they not seen the signs about heavy petting?

I guess the gym is a good enough place as any to meet people with whom you share a common interest. And if you blur your eyes you can imagine what they would look like in their scants.

25TH JANUARY 1998.

"MY ALPHABET FRIEND"

ARTY	MY FRIEND HEM IS LIKE AN ALPHABET SOUP
BELLY BUTTON	AND HE'S GOT A LITTLE FRIEND CALLED LOOPY LOOP
CRAZY	HE IS MY FAVOURITE FRIEND WHO IS A BOY
DONKEY	I WISH THEY'D MANUFACTURED A ~~XXXX~~ TOY!
EROTIC	SO, HERE'S A LITTLE POEM ABOUT MY ALPHABET FRIEND
FAVOURITE	I HOPE YOU DON'T THINK I'M GOING ROUND THE BEND!
GRAPE	HE IS QUITE CREATIVE, I'D SAY HE'S ARTY
HONEY	AND I THINK HE'D LIKE A BELLY BUTTON PARTY!
INFECTIONS	HE'S A CRAZY KIND OF BOY LIKE MY CAT WONKIE
JOLLY	AND SOMETIMES WHEN HE'S MEAN I'M CALLED A DONKEY
KIPPER	EROTIC IS HIS FAVORITE WORD (HE THINKS IT'S FUNNY)
LOVES A LOCKETT	AND MAYBE HE LIKES GRAPES AND HONEY
MELONHEAD	HIS PERSONALITY IS INFECTIONS AND JOLLY
NAUGHTY BOY	AND RATHER THAN A KIPPER I THINK HE'D LIKE A LOLLY.
OVER EASY	HE LOVES A LOCKETT (!), YES, THAT'S ME
PEA BRAIN	ALTHOUGH HE CALLS ME 'MELONHEAD' WHICH I JUST
QUEENY	CAN'T SEE.
RASCAL	SOMETIMES HE'S A NAUGHTY BOY WHO'S RATHER
SWEETIE	OVER EASY
TU TU	SOMETIMES HE'S A PEABRAIN AND THE ONLY THING
UGLY	THAT RHYMES IS CHEESY!!
VEST	HE'S NOT REALLY A QUEENY, I WROTE THAT TO BE MEAN
WALLY	BUT HE'S THE CHEEKIEST RASCAL THAT I'VE EVER SEEN!
XYLOPHONE	HE IS SUCH A SWEETIE AND NOW ONTO TU TU
Y-FRONTS	THERE'S NOTHING THAT RHYMES ABOUT FIONA CHOO CHOO!
ZANEY.	HE'S NOT REALLY UGLY, I SAID THAT IN JEST
	AND I'M NOT QUITE SURE IF HE WEARS A VEST!
	HE IS A WALLY AND PLAYS A XYLOPHONE
	ALTHOUGH THAT'S A SECRET HE'S NEVER SHOWN!
	HAVE YOU GOT A PAIR OF Y-FRONTS? I DON'T KNOW
	BUT YOU ARE SO ZANEY YOU'VE GOT A CERTAIN
	GLOW! X.

We all love a bit of Alpha Beta, whether it's Prince with his street, kids with their spaghetti, or cute cousins in school plays reciting the song 'A you're adorable, B you're beautiful, C you're a cutie full of charms'. In fact, forget the last one, I just listened to it on the internet and it's actually verging on creepy, a bit like that weird Johnny Burnette song that goes, 'You're all ribbons and curls, oh, what a girl, eyes that twinkle and shine, you're sixteen, you're beautiful, and you're mine.' Crrrreeeeeppy. Who is all ribbons and curls at sixteen?

I think this is the nicest note ever (and I've seen a lot of notes). It's funny, clever, and very thoughtful – and must have taken bloody ages to write. I would have given up after F, as I wouldn't have been able to find any words that weren't rude for that.

OK, so it's a little weak in places – Q for Queeny isn't great, but at least the poet admits this, and Xylophone's a bit feeble. But the whole poem is pulled back by the Y-fronts (actually, isn't being pulled back by the Y-fronts called a wedgie? Never mind). The writing looks good as well – all terribly neat and in capitals. In fact, the whole thing shows that this author means business and is determined that the recipient will be bloody happy by the time he gets it. Even if he is a pea brain.

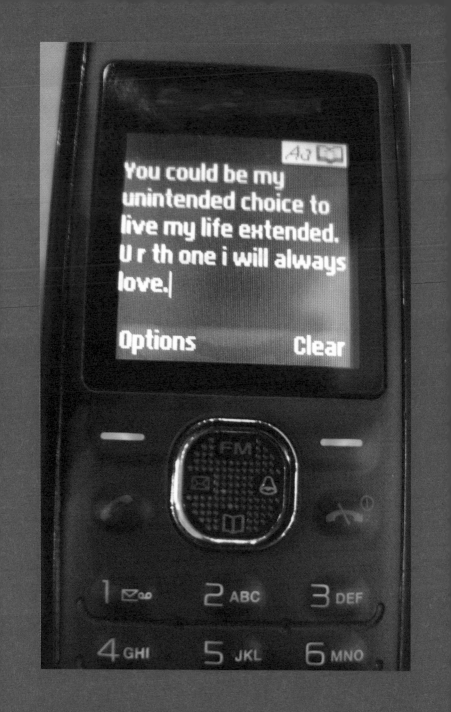

If I had been the recipient of this note, here's what I'd be thinking, 'Well thanks *very* much for this. Your "unintended" ... why? Am I such a crap bet that you could never have seen yourself with me? Am I your sloppy seconds? Was there someone else that you totally intended to be with who just didn't intend to be with you back? And what makes you think you're *my* choice?'

Maybe I'm being harsh. I suppose people do talk about being hit by a bolt of lightning, it all coming out of the blue or being struck by one of cupid's arrows. I suppose love is meant to arrive when you're not looking for it. Maybe that's what they meant by 'unintended'? But, alas, I know the story behind this one and they didn't stay together. I'm sure that wasn't intended when this message was written.

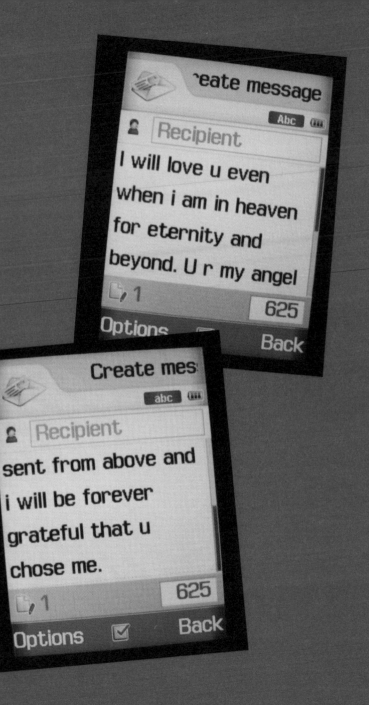

'Even when I'm in heaven'? That's slightly threatening, suggesting ghostly apparitions in the future. I think it's important to make clear early on that if one of you dies, you won't hang around haunting the other, *Wuthering Heights* style, in the name of 'eternal love'. Yes, best to discuss this now, as I presume it's quite difficult to explain that you're not trying to scare the shit out of your loved one by appearing as a spectre in their bedroom!

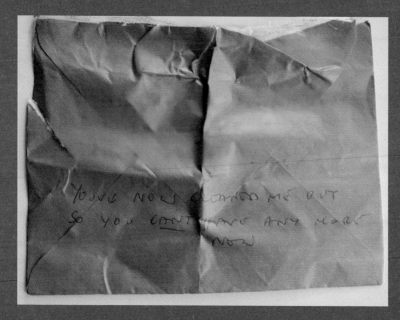

It's one thing to help each other out, but here is a point that no relationship should reach. It's the stage of becoming the pseudo parent. This is a relationship where, instead of going Dutch, you should go and ditch. He/she has become a leech, and whether this means financially, emotionally, or something else, the relationship has become a little lopsided. Unless you're a fully-fledged masochist who likes being used and abused, you should get out of this. There's also nothing that kills passion more than feeling like you need to tell off your other half, or keep bailing them out. The sad thing about this note is the pink envelope. Please don't tell me they had to pay for their own birthday meal, or worse, had to buy their own valentine's card. If they've cleaned you out, you need to get them to clear off.

P.S. my post code has changed to _____ / that means I want a reply. NOW!

If you're looking for an assertive woman, or even a dominatrix, here's your gal. I like her style. No pussy footing around, sitting looking out the window waiting for the postman to arrive. This babe means business, she isn't writing love notes for them to disappear into the ether with not even the meagre courtesy of a reply. I quite like the idea of being told, no, instructed, to write beautiful prose. I have visions of a woman clad in thigh high boots whipping a small, cowering English professor as he frantically writes beautiful soliloquies in his dusty mahogany office. 'Do it, you corduroy-clad crap, write me a beautiful love letter NOW!!!'

I hope you will Not Mind
What I have wrote in this letter
forgive me if I am Wrong. "Sorry"

Be Mine's. I promise.!! NI
I'll make → you Very → Rich If you will

Desperate times lead to desperate measures. I've had to block out a lot of this message, but it's essentially a begging letter. It's quite confusing, and swings dramatically from apologetic pleading to extravagant promises like 'I will make you rich'. Pleading and promises – a dangerous combination.

A Turn for the Worse

Now is the time to take stock of your relationship. The honeymoon period is well and truly over, and you're finding it hard to see past your beloved's annoying habits.

Plus, temptation may have started to rear its ugly head. You've become so comfortable in your relationship that you find yourself with a bit of time on your hands. Idle hands make light work, and from mild flirtations at work to the perils of the Internet, there are many temptations that can trouble even the most steadfast of relationships. While I'm on this subject, let me just warn you about anonymous Internet dating. Having ventured into this in the name of research, I was fairly alarmed by the array of pictures I received – the volume and variety of which I could have used to make an extremely x-rated calendar. My innocent advert seemed to attract a huge number of nutters, but if I had been tempted to stray from my relationship I sure as hell could have, and let's just say I would know exactly what I was getting beforehand.

At this stage in the relationship you might find yourself trying to remember the good times, which are becoming few and far between. If all you can think of are the bad times, then you're going to end up in this section of the book.

This chapter covers the fork in the road, when you either find yourself thinking, 'Wow, this has gone like, *so* wrong …', or you have the, 'This is it. This is the one' moment. We'll address the broken hearts and the failed relationships here, and be warned, there's a fair amount of jealousy, hate and revenge in the following pages. They're all subjects that have become big business, particularly online. There are whole websites dedicated to providing top tips about how to get revenge and to generally ruin someone's life. And yet you can't help feeling that taking this extreme action will only ruin your own chances of finding a new relationship. One sniff of a boiling bunny and the new love of your life will be out the door faster than you can say 'Basic Instinct'. If you aren't looking for revenge but are nonetheless full of seething hate, there is also a website dedicated to getting rid of the gifts your ex gave you, sort of an ex-bay. And then there are the dating sites specifically set up for married people having affairs, which could make for risky surfing. You know you're totally fucked if you go on a site seeking new thrills and meet your other half there, doing the same thing. It would be funnier if this scenario happened in the real world rather than the virtual world, of course, and the cheating couple encountered each other at a speed dating event. You can imagine the competition to see who could say 'you're dumped' the quickest!

It doesn't always have to end acrimoniously, of course – breaking up might not be easy but now and again some people come out of relationships amicably and even manage to stay friends. However, that's generally not the case where indiscretion, an affair, or merely suspicious minds are involved. Of course, you can also bring it on yourself by carrying the excess baggage of a previous relationship into a new one – mentioning the ex in every other sentence and continuously comparing and contrasting. I once heard of someone keeping hold of a sex tape they'd filmed with their ex. Apparently they 'just weren't ready to get rid of it yet'. Surely any saucy documentation relating to a relationship should be destroyed at the point of break up, just in case you find yourself on the pages of 'readers' wives' or worse still, getting 3 million hits on YouTube. Lecture over, relationship over, finito, caput, THE END.

READING BETWEEN THE LINES OF LOVE

Is it me or is this beginning to look a bit doomed?
This is the reading between the lines bit, where things
aren't looking good …

Couldn't help putting the 'honest' on, could you? So near, and yet so far from being nice!

Tried to impress a girl by
taking her to your amazing café
but it was ruddy closed down
R.I.P come back soon

Oh no! There's no excuse for this. If you're trying to win someone over, don't scrimp on lots of logistical work and double checking. Without a spreadsheet and months of military-like planning, what started out as a romantic idea can turn into a grumpy disaster.

To arrive somewhere for your romantic meal to find it closed is unlucky; to find it has shut down is an omen! There's something about writing about your love in public that always seems to jinx it. It's just when you've decided to let the world know you're very happy and think you might even be in love that you find out your partner's been banging someone behind your back.

En Tarentaise, Savoie
·LES MENUIRES (alt 1815 m)
La station et les pistes du Roc des 3
Marches (2700m)

At the moment I am
skiing in val Thorens. The
snow and sun are both
ionsliant but the food isn't.
The oldest boys here are 13.
Our ski instructor fancies
Miss ▒▒▒▒▒ and
▒▒▒▒▒ hurt her knee on
the first day so she hasn
been skiing-she says Hi

Got to go
Love

Young love eh? Always the same story. You go on holiday brimming with excitement – and not just because of the weather, or the respite from the daily grind. It's the potential offered by the new turf – the new, unexplored territory. This might be where you find the love of your life! In years to come you'll reminisce fondly about the skiing holiday where you met and how you weren't expecting it at all. Of course, when you get there a quick survey reveals a severe lack of potential, and the only passable target is guaranteed to be interested in your friend/teacher/whatever. Bollocks.

8th October:

I'm sorry this letter may seem boring
cos I haven't fucked up my life
lately. Sorry!!

In the bar at uni, with my
Pint

Dear

ELLO, cheers for your letter it was really cool
to hear from you. You sound like you're having a bloody
exelent time, which is even better
I am a bit worried that you are going to this
Gay club thing, is there something you're not telling me
uh?!!
I'm really Glad ___ come home, do you
reckon you'll get a chance to go home and see him?
At the moment I'm sitting in the bar cos I

Fucking up is what they make shows about, what agony aunts get employed for, and what gossips at the water cooler get sacked for. It fuels so much discussion – if no one did it, the world would be a truly boring place. In relationships, of course, you try to learn from your mistakes, although sadly there seems to be a large number of us that finds life and relationships a bit boring when everything's sailing along nicely. As a result people sometimes think it's best to stir up a few currents, rock the boat. Scandal, shock, and disgrace generate hard cash. I don't think many of the red tops would sell if their headlines read, 'Kate Moss in wholesome relationship shocker! Model enjoys cooking and jigsaw puzzles!' or 'Amy and Blake happily married, working 9–5, and planning a two-week summer holiday!' No, fuck-ups keep us entertained, drive us on, give us something to think about, and in this case, something to write about.

So? Can't help thinking someone is taking too much of an interest in who or what 'S' likes. Or maybe this is an announcement by 'S' and he's coming out in a big way. He is going to write it on walls and paint the town red. Who knows and who cares? Well, maybe 'S's girlfriend does, if he has one.

One girl's dud is another girl's stud …

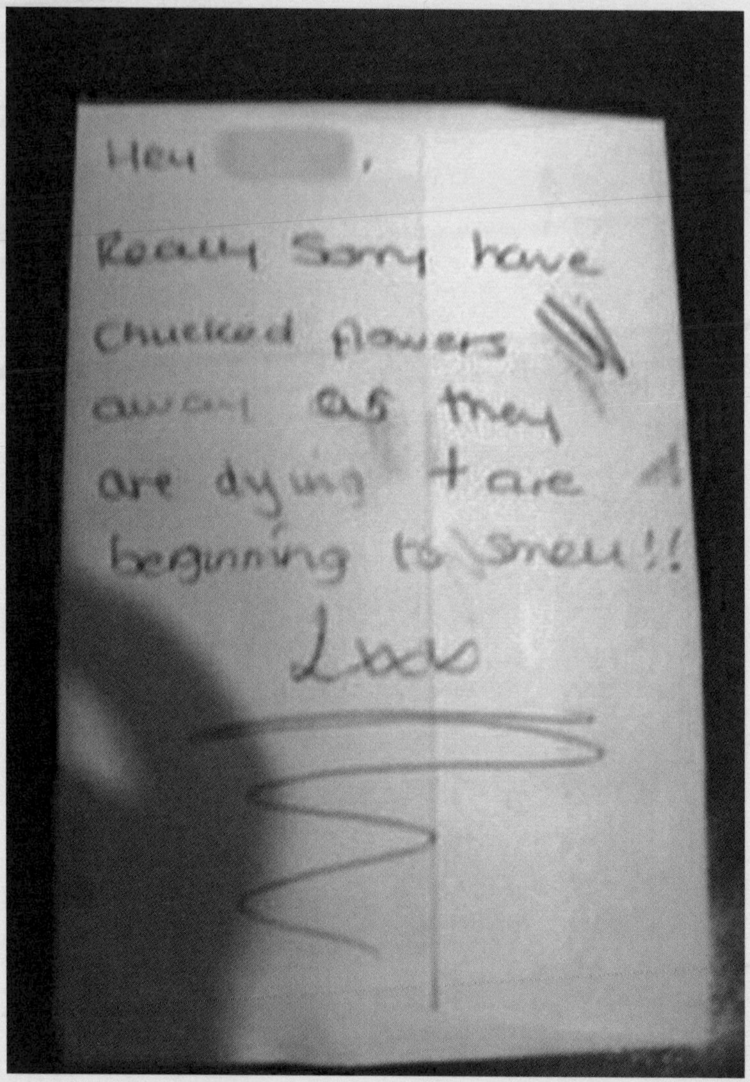

What an arsehole! I get it, you're living in a flat and one of you receives a major, in your face, bouquet from a very fanciable individual. It's probably taken blood, sweat and tears to get them to notice you, never mind send you some flowers. So you put them in a vase, feeling justifiably proud and touched. I think you're allowed to keep them there until they've completely withered and are essentially turning to dust, unless you're some sort of Barbara Cartland or Elton John type who receives flowers every half hour. So someone else deciding when you should stop revelling in your newfound appeal seems a little bit harsh and verging towards jealousy. 'They smell'? This sounds pointed. They might as well say the guy that sent them to you smells and that he should go in the bin too.

The person who sent me this note pointed out that if she turned the tables and started throwing out all of her flatmate's pongy stuff there would be very little left. Sounds as though this bitter flatmate has a touch of the Baby Janes about her – I wouldn't have been surprised if she'd simply cut all the heads off the flowers. I'd watch her closely, and perhaps get on the phone to Interflora and send *her* some flowers to be on the safe side …

and I hope that you can read my writing. I will probably end up phoning you on ~~Sun~~ Sunday night from home or even on Saturday from Aberdeen depending on how bored I am

Yours

R...

Oh right, so *if* you get bored you'll go for the last resort. In other words, me. Seriously, if I'm really that close to the bottom of the barrel then you can shove your phone up your arse …

BABY

You know I love you, but is there one thing you could stop doing? I would have said this in person, but I am late for work. Could you stop getting jam in the butter? It isn't very nice in the morning on my toast. Otherwise, you are perfect.

xoxoxo
♡♡♡

There's a song by comedian Jon Shuttleworth that contains the lyrics: 'Two margarines on the go, it's a nightmare scenario …' It could have been composed especially for the writer of this note. You have old and new margarines in the fridge and someone opens the new one before the old one is finished – aaarrrrggh! Similarly, I can't stand it when someone doesn't properly remove the foil from the peanut butter jar and you spend ages trying to get your knife underneath it just to get a tiny scrape of the stuff … why oh why oh why? There's no need for this – didn't you spot the lid?!

So I do have a bit of sympathy for the author of this note, although I admit it's a little pedantic. The worst bit, though, is the lame and condescending attempt to make up for it with the 'otherwise you're perfect' finish. They might as well have gone for the classic cliché, 'you're sweet enough'. Excuse me while I retch. Back to the point of the note though. While it really is not great having your sweet and savouries mixed in the morning, if this person's biggest crime is butter tainting I wouldn't push my luck and write a note about it. You never know, they might end up sending it to an author who'd make fun of it in a humour book. Perish the thought …

Love is apparently *not* all you need. Money seems to play a large part.

I always start laughing when I think about this cake … in fact, I can only just manage to type this. This is a wedding cake made by a Mexican bakery based in the UK. The mother of the bride, thinking she was a bit too cool for school in her appreciation of other global cultures, decided to place her order in Spanish, instructing the baker to ice the names of the couple on it, telling them the caterers would pick it up on the big day. She boasted about her linguistic talents to the other wedding guests, and waited eagerly to see the finished result. When the cake arrived, lo and behold it had 'Piper y Barbara' beautifully piped on top. How lovely. But, wait a minute … Barbara and Piper? Guess what? Not the bride and groom. Nope. This tasty looking cake turned out to be a bit of free advertising for the bakery. It seems something got a little bit lost in translation, and they dedicated it to themselves. Piper y Barbara. Mexican bakers extraordinaire.

Anyway, apparently it was a very hot day and the mother of the bride kept shrieking that the icing was melting anyway … all the while laughing manically and protesting that it didn't really matter. And I'm sure Piper and Barbara were very touched by such a romantic dedication.

BAD NEWS AND LOST LOVE

Abandon ship! Abandon ship! The relationship's a gonner.
Get your Kleenex at the ready – this part of the book is full
of apologies and unhappy endings.

leaving

Like blood my tears
            fall to the floor.
Your switchblade sharp tongue,
Digs deep into my heart.
The words are cold
With a raw and cutting edge.
They slice through my feelings,
Ripping me apart.
Did you mean what you said?
Are you leaving?
Then twist the knife no more.

In the tortured world of a teenage love, a week-long relationship is the equivalent of one year in an adult one, I reckon. Must be something to do with hormones rampaging around the body, or the excitement of the first flush of love.

To quote Craig David (thankfully, not an everyday occurrence), 'Monday, took her for a drink on Tuesday, we were making love by Wednesday ... ' You know the rest. Unfortunately, more often than not, by Sunday the teenage relationship had come crashing down, the antics of the weekend leaving one of the two wanting out before they were ever in.

This poem is about none of that. How do I know? Sadly, I wrote it. It was written before I had even had a relationship, and was based purely on what I presumed it would feel like at the end of a torrid relationship. It says an awful lot about me that instead of writing steamy poetry or romantic songs, I preferred to write about the devastation at the end of a romance. I should have been a Goth. In fact, if I had been a bit savvier I would have realised that I had a great career in hypothetical romance ahead of me. I could have been the next Barbara Cartland, sitting in a pink feathered dress and writing about manly hands on heaving bosoms. I might just start wearing one while I write this anyway. Better than wearing black and Doc Martens.

on Tuesday and last night. I hope you are not in tears by now and hope that you can read my dreadful writing (although this is my third draft)

Yours sorrowfully

'I hope you're not in tears.' You can't see the rest of this note, and I wouldn't really worry about it. Let's just stay you'd have to have blocked tear ducts *not* to be blubbing. There are some people in the world who enjoy being the harbingers of bad news. The first warning sign is when they come and put an arm around your shoulder so they can get all the gossip. They are a 'friend' when your life is going down the tubes, but less happy when things are looking rosier for you – a frenemy. Any content, happy, confident individual doesn't punch the air every time one of their 'friends' is a bit down on their luck. This note not only brought bad news but seems to have slightly dramatised it, with a nice touch of 'I told you so' thrown in for good measure.

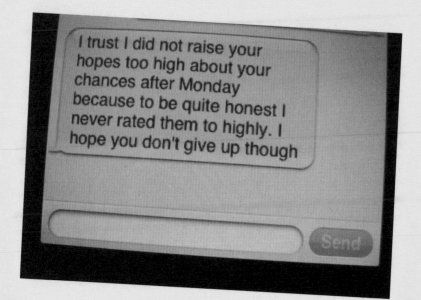

I trust I did not raise your hopes too high about your chances after Monday because to be quite honest I never rated them to highly. I hope you don't give up though

That's helpful, isn't it? It might have been good for them to mention this beforehand, don't you think? Actually, no it wouldn't – who cares or knows the reasons for getting a knock back.

If there's one concept I hate, it's the idea of being 'out of your league' or 'punching above your weight'. Nobody is in any league for God's sake. So what if they have a flash job and a fancy car? What if they have no personality? Every Jack has their Jill, and flash Harry wankers will always find money-grabbing daft birds. Nice people will always find each other. So if you get a knock back you obviously just haven't met someone in the same nice 'league' as you.

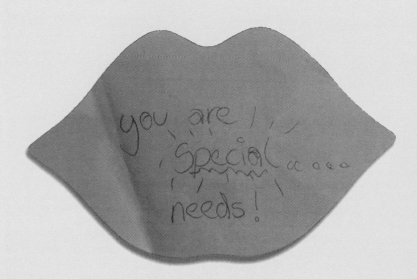

Isn't that sweet. Starts out as a bit of a cliché and turns into a little quip. This must have been from one of those hilarious characters who thinks farting on to your hand proves they love you.

While I'm writing, could you pass on a message to [redacted] tell her that the Cheltenham or the Abbey National are her best bets

Thanks

Just a big

Sorry!

to apologise for causing you unnecessary trauma over ye past two years! Should have realised much earlier that I was born to be single [redacted]

Born to be single ... I think this fellow speaks the truth. Whatever he did to end the relationship in the first place, I'm sure that if his ex was plagued by any lingering heartbreak, it was swiftly replaced by relief when she saw this charming note. You're better off out of a relationship with a man who doesn't know that 'I'm sorry' notes are not the place to discuss building society accounts.

plutonic

platonic.

The possibility and the potential are there, but the harsh reality is it's just not meant to be. If you can finish a relationship and remain friends, or have a friendship that turns into a relationship before turning back into a friendship, then you've met a truly special companion, and what's more you're an incredibly sensible, mature and well balanced person. In fact you should start running classes.

The background to this note is really interesting. These two – a male and a female – were friends for many years before one night the inevitable happened and they had a drunken snog. This letter is in response to the subsequent, 'Shit, what now?' moment. The note is lovely and diplomatic. It mentions that although the author was 'rat arsed', they did remember the snog, but it also says they don't feel any different and as they are such good friends, they don't want to lose that friendship. An awkward situation sorted as best it could be – it would be sad to lose a friendship over a drunken fumble.

The best bit about this note is this scribble on the back. Don't you sort of wish they'd gone with 'plutonic'? 'I think it's best if our relationship remains plutonic …' Puts a whole different spin on things, doesn't it?

She could cause hurricanes with just the blink of her eye lids
I could stand there and with stand the winds she brings

She could tell me a thousand lies
I would believe every one of them

She could hold my heart within her palms
I would gladly count the lines on them

She could say the worst of the worst to me
My anger wouldn't be able to compete with the love I have for her

She could make enemies with my soul alone
I would still take her side and fight myself if I had to

I could watch a thousand deaths and not flinch
She could tell me two things and have me die inside

I could hold onto her until the hands on the clock begin to ache
She could make me want to ache that much more

I could have all the money the world could give
She could make me want to trade it all for just a moment with her

She could be gone for one tenth of a millisecond
I would miss her intently

If only I could be what she wanted, I would be that much happier, the loss of a love is the
worse thing anyone can go through, they say there is nothing like your first love, they are
right. If I could meet them I would tell them how much she means to me.

It would definitely be an understatement to say that 'she' made an impression on the author of this poem. While researching this book I received a lot of stuff that just isn't printable – I think some of it might be etched on to my brain forever (people are strange, and what they want done to them is even stranger). Yet some of the material I've received has been so very sweet that it's made me believe in the human race again. This poem is particularly heartrending. Writing something like this can be quite cathartic, and a healthy way of moving on. Poetry can also be dangerous though: things can get a bit full on, verging on the obsessive.

I've also received a lot of stuff written by people whose obsession seems to be with being *in love*, rather than the person they are supposed to be *in love with*. It can be addictive, apparently, being in love. We all know people who jump from one relationship to another – each one as extreme and intense as the last. It's understandable really, the adrenalin from a relationship can be inspiring. Many a song has been born out of love, or a love lost. I hope 'she' and he get together.

The very least I owe you is an apology, not for the way things stand but for the
way and the cowarduos route i choose to bring us to this juncture.
No one deserves to be treated in such a callous and selfish, least of all one who
has brought joy and compaionship intoo my life. For this I will be eternal sorry.

Words seem to be failing me at this point , but honestly I true never meant in the
way I inevitable have.
I find it hard to believe that I would put my unease at making a phone call in
front of feelings of one i care so much about.
Maybe within that sentence is the reason why but still, it is no excuse.

Is there a great big reason why it happened, did something suddenly change. The
only answer I can give is no there wasn't any great noticeable change. The only
one I can give is, and believe me its awful but unfortuanatley I am who I am, is
it's been a repeated pattern any time that something starts to evolve that
contains any kind of commitment I seem to bail. LAME!
The short of it is that I feel that I can't be in a long distance relationship
with someone.
you know yourself its hard, at times it almost soul destroying.
Quite possible it could be my well oiled defense system that seems to spring from
nowhere and only leave regrets.
To this only time will tell, but I can't change way I think or feel.
I know to me you will always speacil a little bit crazy alittle bit mad, but with
a heart and character so big and colourful it consumes and refreshes all. I know
this past five months have been hard but every anguished thought was clouded out
by sense of joy and anticipation. I was happy and extemely happy and that still
under plays it, for that I will be eternal great, that is a gift I fear I will
never be to return in kind.
Despite all this i think, I feel things have to change, I can't carry on the
thinks were/are. Sight, smell taste ,touch are important sense wow that seems
awful but that is how I'm feeling. I'm not explaining myself very,much liike
scrambled garbage silence opn the phone.

I shall leave it here for now, saying I don't ask for, want, or deserve your
forgiveness, but I do hope we can salvage some kind of friendship which will
hopefully bear some good times some where down the line.

I`m so sorry

I just can't read this – it makes me want to cry, or at least shout 'Brace! Brace! We're going to crash!' I've been really touched by how honest and brave some people have been in giving me material for this book. This is from one of those people.

One of the worst things about this entry is that you can totally see where it's all going. In the grand scheme of things, perhaps it isn't the worst break up note in the world, but it would be better never to have to get any break up notes at all. At least there's a clear admission from the author that they're being a coward. There are also a few nice comments – although I think being called 'colourful' often means 'I think you're totally bonkers'. For the record, I want to point out that I think bonkers is incredibly good. Why have bland when you can have barmy? I'm sure this colourful character won't be alone for long.

on, I don't think its right going through ████ all the time, even though this letter is coming through ████ (Ha, Ha). Anyway I think I'll leave it at that.

See ya
luv

I don't know what I expect to achieve from this letter but I think its best we try and sort things out. I never was very good at saying what I wanted to say to you. I think letters are sometimes the cowardly way out but I'm not feeling too strong at the moment. As you probably have heard I know what happened. I think its a shame I had to hear it from ████ and not directly from you, but I know this is hard for you too. You know I actually keep kidding myself that maybe you'll change your mind or something, then again I can't say I really know what I'm feeling at the moment. I don't know how you felt about me coz you never expressed any emotion apart from when you were pissed or stoned. I never said anything but that certainly made me feel used and unsure of your feelings towards me. As you know I really cared for you, you could say loved you, but how can you love someone who gives nothing in return and my feelings towards you aren't going to overnight like your feelings towards me have. I wish I had your strength to pick things up and carry on, but things don't happen that easy for me.

I don't really care if you screw this letter up and laugh at least in letting you know how I feel, very hurt to put it bluntly. look, I'm not looking for sympathy or anything, just maybe the truth to get things straight. I'd like it if you could let me know (on paper if you like) exactly whats going

There's an interesting story behind this letter, which was written over a decade ago during those emotional school years. The young lady is asking why the gentleman is not more interested in her, and wants to know what's happening, what's going on? The gentleman who gave me the letter was a walking answer, though. He turned into the fabulous Russella, drag queen extraordinaire. (If you don't believe me go to www.russella.co.uk.)

08/06/06

Hi! Its late! I'm tired! I've got an exam tomorrow but I've got to communicate with you somehow or else I'll never be able to get to sleep!

You've let me get really really attached to you, its unfair of you to have done it! that letter you wrote, the one you wouldn't give me because it made it too embarrassed, you said that I was somehow different or made you feel different & I was special to you I never felt different or special or that you cared about me in the slightest (although common sense disproved this notion) but suddenly, that night we got really caned in years) it dawned on me that you really did care, that even though when you wrote that you loved me I'd never believed you and suddenly I thought well maybe he does in one way or another But now, you've made me feel, like

a fool for believing you. Its unfair to compare you to but he made a fool of me in the same way. He said things that made me love him then denied them all in one fell swoop!

I do understand exactly how you want things to be but I don't think I want it to be that way. Neither do I want this to finish but I find that you don't like to compromise its either "all" or "nothing" with you OK so were neither of us going to stop getting off with other people, its stupid to say that at our age, sexual appetites vary from person to person but you can safely say that we're basically on the sexual market and sub-consciously its everyone's aim to get off with as many people as possible before its too late (for what? I dare not even contemplate) But its always good to have

one anchor safely down, one person
you can feel entirely safe with, you can
do anything you want & not worry if
they don't want it too... because you
know without doubt that they do!
Someone who you don't have to lie or
pretend to. Honesty can be so simple &
such a f relief, to the system!
I felt as if I could be honest with you but
Suddenly I'm all worried about whats
going to happen and paranoia is completely
strange to me as I've never ever worried
what you ~~thought~~ thought of me & to be
quite honest I don't like it maybe I sound
like a spoilt child who wants everything
to be fair and easy, who ~~gong~~ it all
her own way but really I basically just
want you to want me too!
A Bientôt.

Take a look at this old chestnut. It's the old, 'I couldn't help it, I think
it's healthy to see other people, maybe we have different sexual
appetites, maybe we should have an open relationship' line. This
young lady should quit while she's ahead ... just because you have
a big appetite doesn't mean you need to satiate it.

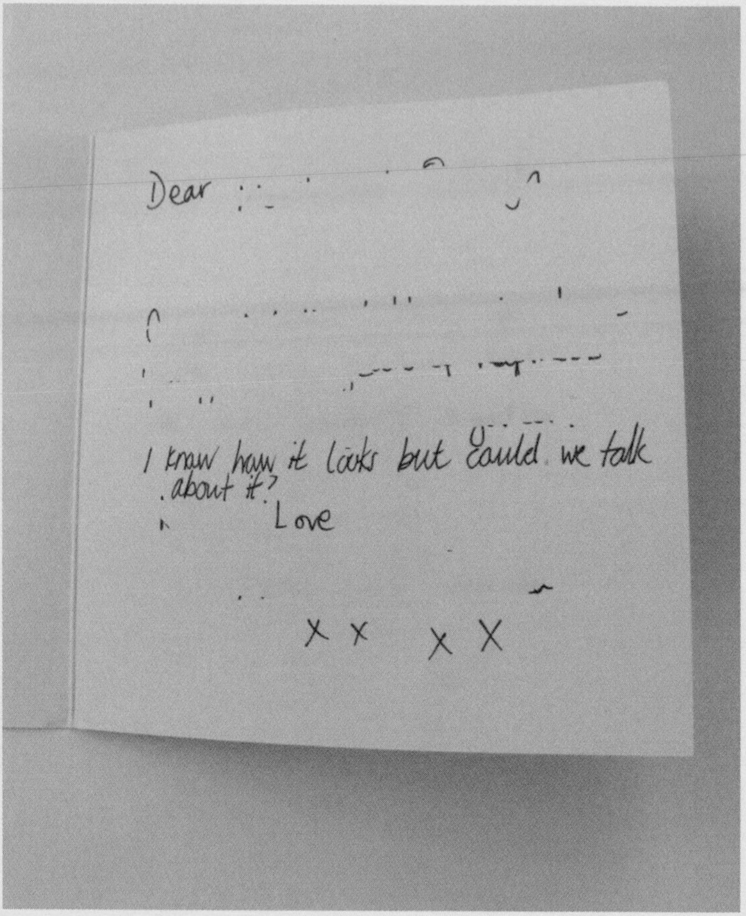
Dear
I know how it looks but could we talk about it?
Love
X X X X

It's often worth giving someone the benefit of the doubt, once. No more than once, mind, as after that you might find yourself being renamed 'the carpet'. It can be very hard to trust someone, and as this is the basis of most relationships, putting yourself in a situation where 'how it looks' could be misinterpreted is just stupid.

Guest Check

TABLE NO.	PERSONS	WAITER	CHECK NO.
			050881

	AMOUNT

bitch huh.
But! It's true, I bet g
think. What's the point??
Seriously! Have gone away —
I'm coming back — but I'll
be away again too.
Look. Well! I don't know
whether I'm saying we should
forget this — "us". Sometimes I
wonder like — is there an
us??
But even if that
what I'm saying
so not what I want

Tops 45701

This seems to be an example of that automatic writing thingy that the surrealists did – where you write and instead of it being conscious thought, it kind of emerges from you as if you were in some sort of trance. I think that roughly translates as 'the rubbish you write when you've had too many shandies'. This is a very sweet note, although it's a bit sad too. It seems to be asking lots of questions, many of which are rhetorical. In this situation the only thing for it is to write a pros and cons list, and if the only thing on the pros list is that your partner doesn't smell … well, then you have your answer.

Hiya Lovey.

Just thought I'd drop you a line if you can phone me for no reason then I should be able to manage a page of babble too!

Sex, yes well weird subject that, don't know why people find it so fascinating. After all it's just something you do, however great it feels its not like its some great act of courage, bravery, individuality or any of the other good qualitees or qualities in human nature what I was in the middle of saying when I so rudely had to dash off to the doctor (nothing exciting either as it turned out just a course of anti-biotics) was just that maybe I've given the "impression, it may seem like I don't really rate sex but I do actually think its cool and especially with someone you know well (that isn't a hint by the way) because you don't worry about telling them what to do. And also maybe I do think its something special as I find myself wanting to do it with just any old person either but mainly because I just can't be bothered to give waste my time concentrating on giving them an orgasm when I know they probably won't have the consideration to do the same for me. Like with for example, he thinks that we don't have sex so often any more is because there's no opportunity but the truth of the matter is I would make opportunities its just that he's just so

damn selfish that I'm sick of him. I'm working on turning into a sex-starved maniac so that every time he sees me he's just burning with desire (ahem) but maybe it's just push him away oh well. I'm tired of thinking about it I just want to feel safe about him so I can comfortably play around with you! Its cool, I think, that this "no strings" side of our relationship is working so well I definitely think we should "be in it" go for it! Its as I said, cool! (also major ego boost!) My only regret is I feel so two-faced. I'm comforting her & telling her you're not worth getting so upset about when I don't mean half of it. I just don't know what else to do. She doesn't need me to have cheated on her too!

I was so embarrassed at lunchtime when I was going on about me getting off with other people. It made me sound like a complete whore who is totally unusual and cheats on her boyf. Which is completely & utterly wrong! says it's perfectly fine to do it & I shouldn't feel ashamed & I don't but the scary thing is that with the other people I've been with while seeing I never felt guilty in the slightest it was if it wasn't even cheating but with you it felt & like I was having a total fling thing which I've decided is bad and good and yes fun so just shut your mouth about me all enjoying it. Since I stopped conveying any useful information shortly after the date I'll just do some German television instead.

Affairs might suit some people, but in this instance it doesn't sound like all parties concerned are happy. Yes, this is an affair that is definitely going to have a messy end. A discussion's already underway about guilt and no guilt so I guess she subconsciously knows it's coming. Losing the lazy boyfriend who is only interested in his own orgasms seems fair enough – leave him to it then he can orgasm as often as he wants, he sounds like a right wanker – but betraying the friend could make things nasty.

MEET ME AT THE
ELEVATOR IN SMINS!
X:

It all seems so terribly exciting at first: clinches in corridors, eroticism in elevators … You feel like someone in one of those French films, the arty but ever so saucy kind. I just hope the meeting in the elevator didn't affect anyone else, particularly if it was taking place in the initial stages of an exciting relationship. It's bad enough when someone farts in a lift, never mind starts getting their rocks off.

I also hope there's nothing dodgy going on here. I used to take the same train every evening, and as I went down the stairs to get on the underground, the same couple would be kissing passionately in a tucked away corner of the station. I'd walk past them at least once a week and often thought how romantic it seemed – just like *Brief Encounter*! And then I started to wonder about the location they always chose for their clinch. Why the train station? Why so tucked away? They appeared to see each other so regularly and it began to strike me as a little odd that they were always so passionate – kissing as though they were leaving each other for the last time. Of course, it dawned on me one day that this was not exhibitionism but an affair (… just like *Brief Encounter*, I suppose). They were trying (badly) to ensure that nobody saw them, before getting on their separate trains back to their other halves. All a little less romantic …

WHAT?!? You think writing this on a card with a cutesy dog on it is going to soften the blow, do you? What the hell have you spent all my money on? Oh wait a minute, this is a very cute picture so perhaps I'll forgive you … what's a few thousand pounds between friends, after all?

To

Enclosed is my suicide note I doubt
I'll kill myself. I'm to scared to.
▓▓▓▓ is the biggest creep ever
and I hate him well no I fancy him. I♡
him and hate him if that makes sense.
Everything in my note is true.
Why is life so fucking crap I hate it why
can't life be easy? Why can't life be simple?
Why do men always ruin my life?
I have nearly killed myself over ▓▓▓▓

I need to talk to both of you by
yourselves I need to talk to ▓▓▓ but I'll
do that 2marrow.

Thanks for listening to me.

Luv

X

This will be the only time you'll ever read a suicide note and laugh ...
I hope. The teenage years can be very difficult, and this young lady
has obviously had it. Even though she's sick of men and has decided
that this is the end, she's very courteous, thanking the two recipients
of the letter for listening. And given that she goes on to make plans
to speak to them the following day, perhaps we ought not to take her
threats too seriously. I thought she didn't want any more tomorrows?
See? Life and love aren't all that bad.

NO LOVE/HATE

This part of the book is full of expletives and exclamation marks. There's no point mincing your words if you've got some hating to do. If you're feeling vicious then read this, the 'certainly no love lost here' section. Go on, get it off your chest you t**t!

Oh, what a tangled web we weave. You meet someone, you like them, and you think it could all be good. Then you realise they're already taken. What do you do? Have a go anyway? Give up? Or test the waters by sending something anonymously? Hell yeah, let's go for the anonymous option! This little card, attached to a beautiful rose, was delivered to one lucky lady on Valentine's Day. She was doubly chuffed as her boyfriend, though lovely, was not big on romantic gestures, so she knew he must really like her if he'd gone to all this trouble. She immediately set off to his house to thank him, and he opened the door to be greeted by a deluge of hugs and kisses. The boyfriend was a little baffled at such a big show of affection, but thinking his luck was in he wasn't exactly going to look a gift horse in the mouth. Unfortunately it all unravelled when he took the same gift horse upstairs and she muttered in his ear how much she loved the rose and the card. What rose? What card? What the fuck? Who's sending you flowers? What the fuck have you been up to? And so on. I'm told she never did find out who the flower was from (although she had her suspicions), but she knew one thing: it wasn't from the boyfriend.

Dear [name],

I'm writing this letter to say how sorry I am about last week. I know it must have come as a shock and I didn't handle it very well. Know that I never meant to hurt you and I hope everything was OK at the clinic. I am sorry to have put you through that. But [name], just as the bridge on this photo is obscured by the fence, I have obscured more details from you. Early on in our relationship, I slept with 3 other women. I still feel terrible about this but —

3rd January [year]

it was before we were serious about each other. [name], I know that if we were to stay together now, we'd be together for a very long time — possibly forever — but you are too young & inexperienced to make that commitment.

You may never want to speak to me again but I hope you will get over that & stay in touch.

I am so sorry

love [name]

The end of a relationship can be heartbreaking, but at least sometimes you're left with fond memories. Unfortunately, there may be other times when you're left with something else. It's not something you tend to advertise, but I've had several people confide in me that they were left with more of a love hangover than a love note, in the form of a good old STD.

I've found out a bit about the story behind this note. The gentleman who wrote it split up with the girl a week before and mentioned at the same time that he might have given her an STD. Classy guy. In fact, so classy that this note was accompanied by an artistic photograph of a partly obscured bridge, the analogy being that he had obscured some things from her in the relationship. There's nothing worse than having to take a trip to the GUM clinic while you're still in the midst of the weeping and gnashing of teeth that accompany the end of a relationship. (The young lady no longer has the picture of the bridge and thankfully never had the STD.)

If und[...]ld pleas[...]rn to:
PO Box[...]114 Londo[...] E1 8HL

COULD YOU FORWARD THIS TO YOUR
LYING, CHEATING, WHORE OF A DAUGHTER WHO IS
NO DOUBT SUNNING HERSELF SOMEWHERE EXOTIC

PEFC
PEFC/16-33-70
promoting sustainable forestry

I always thought the phrase was 'beware a woman scorned', but this note came from a wounded male. I think sending 'hurt' mail is, pretty much without exception, a very bad idea. Above all, leaving a hateful note means that no matter how well you eventually move on, the other party will always have written evidence of how nutty you once were. There's a chance it will become something you can live with, and maybe even laugh about in the future ('Ha ha, remember when I called you a stupid bitch because you broke my heart?'), but it's more likely to come back to haunt you.

The major problem with this particular note is that it was sent to the loved one's mum. Getting parents involved is always a bit dicey. Let's face it, informing a mother what a shit of a child they have spawned is pretty low, and probably only satisfying for a nanosecond, after which the sender realises the recipient probably doesn't share their views.

An even lower step than sending mail to the family of your ex is deciding to make 'friends' with one of them. It can appear innocent enough at first glance, but it's downright suspicious if an ex-boyfriend suddenly wants to hang tight with your dad in the pub, or makes the odd call to him just looking for his opinion on some trivial matter. With girls, this behaviour usually takes the form of writing notes to the ex's mum, and sending flowers on her birthday. When a vicious ex suddenly becomes all caring and sharing, it's pretty clear they're not quite ready to move on. The lesson here is simple: don't become friends with the family, you'll just be regarded as a bad smell hanging around, but one which most people are too polite to say anything about.

Exes' parents can be equally as bad though, as they can harbour 'issues' with you even if the ex themselves has moved on. The type of mother, for instance, who thinks it necessary to underline how successful and, even more oddly, fertile her offspring are! You should fully expect to receive your ex's most up to date CV and recent wage slips in the post with this sort.

Jemma

You're a dick!

There is something particularly insulting about calling a woman a dick, or any other form of male genitalia. Likewise, a bloke being a fanny seems a particularly effective cuss. But I can't help thinking in this instance, 'dick' might be a term of endearment. Rather than being spat out in your face, it has been lovingly written on a piece of paper, like a proper love token to be immortalised in a book. She is now going to be a dick for ever.

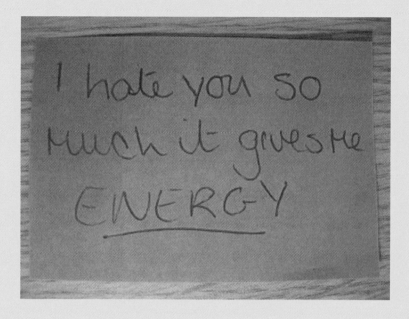

I'm a bit scared of this note. It's the written equivalent of a Scalextric, wheels spinning, ready to fly off the starting grid. This is beyond 'I'm fed up', even beyond 'I'm going to cut up your clothes'. This sounds more like 'I'm going to cut up your face …'

Hate is rarely an attractive look, which I think is what makes this note even scarier. The writer has gone beyond worrying about coming across as weird, bitter or jealous – this person is proud to be a bunny boiler. This is the kind of missive that could spark a generations-long feud – I wonder if it's from a broken-hearted mafia member? Getting embroiled with someone like this is obviously unwise, but you can't always tell straightaway whether someone's normal or a functioning lunatic. But if you get a message like this, it's clear they are not going to give up until you're ruined. Best make sure you have your will in order. You is going down, man!

Block 4

Home of the worlds largest
TURD!

Another charmer, and another highbrow subject … That said, you know a relationship is solid when you can break wind in front of your partner without thinking it's game over, but surely this is taking things a bit far. No need!

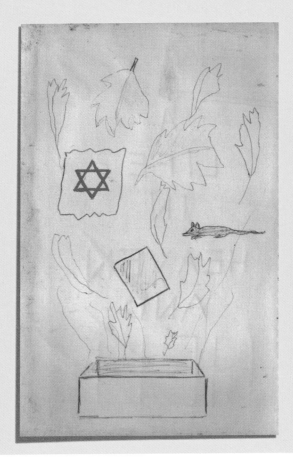

This is like one of those sketches they do in criminal courts because they can't take photos. To quote the person who gave this to me, it is a re-creation of 'easily the best mental parcel I have ever received'. The drawing (due to shock they didn't think of taking a photograph at the time, but drew this lovely sketch) is of a dead mouse in a box, which was left on the gentleman's car by his ex. He did mention that though it happened a long time ago, he knew where the ex lived if I wanted to meet her. I declined the offer for obvious reasons, she is hambonkers.

Would you want to know why someone broke up with you? Not knowing, or not understanding why, is possibly the first sign that the communication in a relationship wasn't perfect. Sometimes it can really come out the blue, or you get the classic excuse of 'it's not you, it's me'. Yet sometimes it really is them. Like with the guy I once dated whose jaw clicked as though it was dislocating every time we kissed – I lived in fear that his mouth would either open like a snake eating an egg, and I'd be consumed, or that it would lock open. There wasn't a hope in hell that when we broke up I was going to mention one of the factors being their creepy dislocating snake jaw … Some things are best left unsaid.

Other times it's achingly obvious why everything has come to an end: infidelity, clash of personalities, whatever. This note is certainly something like that. It's a declaration not only of hatred, but hatred of absolutely anything in the other person's life, which is verging on the terrifying. The recipient must have done something truly vile to deserve this note. If not, the person who wrote this is as mad as a hatter and best to get shot of anyway!

Well, this isn't going to make it into your 'top ten notes you wish you had received' list, is it?

met him
working in the
museum where
she was serving
tea.

Big hands but
nothing down
below.

You know what they say about men with big feet … (they have to wear big shoes). This note will destroy decades of work by women trying to convince men that they don't really talk about them, and specifically that they definitely don't talk about them in any anatomical detail. Alas, in the same way that men talk about girls' attributes, some, and I emphasise some, women do the same. As you can see, the note writer here was obviously a little disappointed that the man who had large hands was not so large elsewhere. Like an announcement in a chain store lift, this man was definitely going down, pressing zero for the underwear department. Perhaps this lady should be careful about who she chooses to discuss this man's attributes (or lack thereof) with, as she'll feel a tad silly if she ultimately falls for Mr Big Hands after announcing to all her friends that he is not Mr Big Pants. I just hope he isn't writing the equivalent note about her.

It is difficult not to resort to cheap jibes at the end of a relationship. To maintain a dignified silence, especially when you're being slagged off to anyone who will listen, is tricky. It's also difficult if you feel you know the other side of your ex's character, and although they might seem like a friendly individual to a casual onlooker, you know they're really a prize wanker.

So here's the answer: just leave some drawings of them around the place! For example, although Miss X might appear to be an intelligent, beautiful young woman, the truth (according to this drawing) is that she's got bingo wings and is known as the wee wee girl. Nuff said.

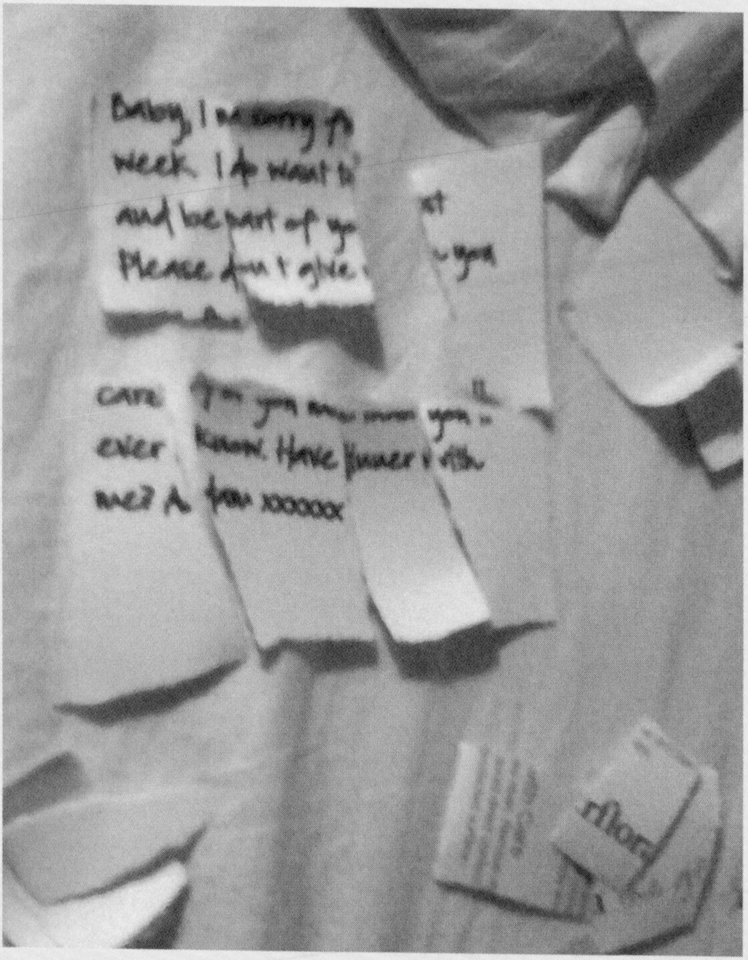

I guess the first sign that this note doesn't necessarily signify the end is that they kept the pieces of the note torn up in a moment of rage. It's difficult to decipher but the bits that I can read say:

'Baby, I'm sorry ... '
' ... week I do want to ... '
' ... and be part of your life ... '
' ... care for you more than you'll ever know ... '

Reading between the lines (and the rips and tears), this was a genuine sorry. And I'm told that not only was the note put back together, but so was the relationship. A happy ever after, for once.

Things Can Only
Get Better and
Happy Endings

'But I love you shitless!' was, believe it or not, the line that won back the ex of a friend of mine. That doesn't exactly sound like a winning line to me, but if you know someone well enough, you'll know how to win back their shitless heart.

This is the alternative option to the break-up – the possible happy ending. In fact, it can be a new beginning. And of course, having broken up you can enjoy making up. You've proved you can take the rough with the smooth, the 'for worse' with the 'for better'. There may have been a few doubts along the way, but you made it through and you're going to stick together like glue from now on. It might have started at chapter one as just a thought, a chance meeting, or a note from a secret admirer but now you're together, and proposals, stag-dos (and don'ts), and even weddings could be in the air. You can remove your make up after a night out, safe in the knowledge that your beloved will still be there in the morning.

You may find some grovelling, some apologies, and some definite compromises in the following pages, but it's probably the most important part of the book. Whatever has gone before has been forgotten and the future is bright (and, crucially, realistic).

Farts, fights and other flaws aside, you're going to accept their faults and remain the Jack to their Jill. You will not only be with them, but also enhance them. Why? Because you love them and while you'll feel safe and secure, you'll no longer be smug, as you have begun to appreciate that a relationship is fragile and has to be kept the 'right way up'. Basically, you're going to love them shitless.

LONG DISTANCE LOVE

This is for all you Shirley Valentines out there.
Does absence makes the heart grow fonder? Or is it out of sight,
out of mind? Bah! Decide for yourself ... these are the notes
from your long haired lovers in, er, Lanzarote.

Hello Love —

Thank you for your letter — It was a important for me; I remember your blue eyes with passion, a sweet passion & your beautiful smile & laugh.

Your eyes are what? Poison? As in, they're going to give you convulsions, make you break out into a sweat and start retching? Great. This is a true lost in translation moment. Any Shirley Valentines out there might recognise this kind of letter, written in the broken English of a holiday romance. Not that I've got anything against these – instead of poor accommodation, dire food and appalling company, you have romantic walks on the beach, meals at sunset and photos to share with everyone when you get back. Alas, photos and memories are all you're left with usually – unless you're particularly unlucky and come back with something only a dose of antibiotics will cure.

So the recipient of this letter is lucky to have received anything, let alone something that makes some degree of sense. Yes, a holiday romance is good if you want one, but if you don't, there's nothing worse than being hounded by someone with only a few teeth but lots of confidence. It's worth doing a bit of research to limit the chances of this happening – if you don't know the local culture, striding out in anything less than a full caftan and scarf can mark you out as the newest hooker in town. My friend went on a donkey ride on holiday and didn't realise the animal's elderly male owner would be joining her. Yes, that's right, sitting behind her, putting his hands round her waist and sometimes also helpfully 'protecting' her breasts. She's convinced it was because she was wearing leggings, which was apparently the equivalent of being totally naked in their culture, so she had to admit it was her own fault. Still, it took the shine off the experience a little.

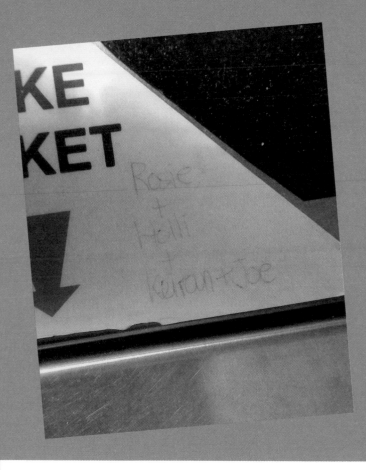

This is weird on so many levels. If you look closely, you'll realise it's written in biro (hardly the tool of a professional graffiti artist), on a ticket barrier at a train station. It might make slightly more sense if the author were professing their passion for their one true love, in which case writing on ticket machines would be fine, along with shouting from the rooftops. But this person (who appears to be at a rather tender age given the handwriting) is so unsure of themselves they've written THREE names! They're either hedging their bets or involved in some sort of juvenile love triangle.

Dearest   ,

            called ..... please tell her when
you get home to say . we home etc she
just called to see how you are .... Oh and
to say " she loves you " (☹) !!

            Regards

                        xxx

Remember the saying 'a face only a mother could love'? Well, you never know if it might apply to you, so perhaps you'd better give her a call …

Relationships are so much easier now that we have mobiles. I remember the days when the only way I could have a private conversation with my boyfriend was by heading to the phone box armed with a fiver's worth of 10 pence pieces. The logistics of dating were tricky before the arrival of mobile phones as well, as there was no way of telling someone you hadn't stood them up but were stuck in traffic. I can't say I miss phone boxes, with their stack of calling cards for busty blondes, and the necessity of breathing through your mouth so you couldn't smell tramps' piss. This also had the added problem of making you sound like a heavy breather, which can be a problem when you're trying to confess your undying love to someone.

"Darling" in spanish. I hope receiving notes from you soon you can write me to some sexy things as well sometimes I loved that very much. I finish this small letter with my foto as you asked me.

here From you soon

Besos XXX

cle

Long distance relationships with lovers from foreign lands can be very romantic. You cherish every letter, pore over every word, and savour the moment before opening a new envelope. Of course, when you open that envelope there's rather a lot of potential for confusion. This young Spanish Romeo has kept things quite simple – in return for teaching his new lady the Spanish for 'darling' he'd simply like some sexy notes.

The fraught flicking of translation dictionaries can be heard the world over after the summer holidays. As with our Latin lover here, half the enjoyment of a foreign affair comes from the fact that you have to keep everything quite basic, cutting out the small talk and getting to something that's universally understood pretty swiftly. Watch out though, as once the novelty of not knowing what your beloved is on about wears off, it's not just the English that can end up broken.

red !! ♡ ☆ ♡
spread l♡ve
red is a loud color. it's the opposite of blue. ⚐ ☆ ☆ ☆☆☆
five points :o:
$money is a serious problem

Simple but true, this message. Red will always be the colour truly associated with love – anything else is just confusing. I doubt that when Sarah Brown met Gordon, she shouted about her love of brown from the rooftops. You'd get a reputation, wouldn't you? Similarly, if you were to express a love of green you would raise a few eyebrows about your attitude to recreational drugs, while loving blue just suggests you sit on your tod reading jazz mags. No other colour is as passionate, or as dangerous, or as loud as red, as the note says. When you first fall in love it does feel loud – it fills your mind, your body, and is in your face all the time. I like the bit about money, too – at least the author's a realist about the future!

This is a very endearing note, mainly, again, because of the 'lost in translation' element. I don't think it's a love note – more of an advert for an assistant (or a wife?). In any event it shows a huge amount of dedication, loyalty, and even passion. The whole tone of the note indicates an overwhelming desire to please. This person will not just help out, not just clean, but will even try to understand and use the often baffling comedic tool of irony. In fact, if you look up the word irony it says: a. *The use of words to express something different from and often opposite to their literal meaning.* Maybe this whole advert is a piss take, and the author has no desire to help at all. If you do hire this person watch out – you'll fall in love with their sarcasm and wit, and will probably end up doting on them hand and foot. They were meant to come and serve you but you end up worshipping them. Oh, the irony!

My pen wrote this,
but my heart dictated it
"I Love You!"

This is just lovely. No need for a note with this notepaper. It looks like it has come from a bygone era, when people wooed each other and Doris Day was racy. Does anyone woo any more?

SICKLY SWEET LOVE

Ugh. This section will make you feel sick, like listening to
a Snow Patrol song. Or, if you like Snow Patrol, it'll probably
leave you feeling all cuddlywuddly inside …

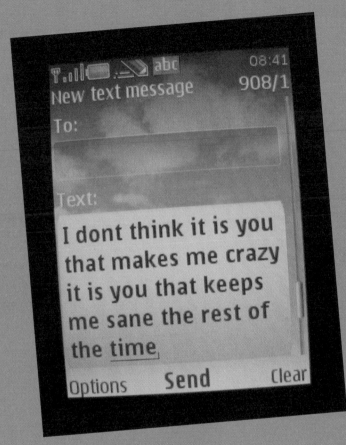

I dont think it is you that makes me crazy it is you that keeps me sane the rest of the time

If you want to check your own sanity go to the note about the dead mouse in the box and decide if you think that is a totally acceptable action after being dumped. Yeah, you don't make me crazy, I'm crazy already.

I'm not a parent but I can only guess that not only is it lovely to get a note like this, but it's also a relief to learn that after all the late nights of nappy changing and feeding, your offspring actually likes you, let alone loves you. That said, it does look as though it's been written on the inside of a toilet roll. I guess it doesn't really matter where you have your eureka moment.

XpressMusic
15:31
I've given you my
heart and soul
please cherish them
forever. X
Options
Reply
Back

Yep, try not to break anyone's heart, or indeed stamp on it, screw it up, or generally destroy it. A good heart these days is hard to find. Did I really just quote Feargal Sharkey?

A note that initially seems lovely, but becomes a bit unnerving with further thought. Are they saying that by keeping them in touch with reality, their beloved is actually a little bit of a Captain Sensible? Do they ask if you have paid the gas bill while you're in the middle of a passionate kiss? Do they warn you that the cupboards weren't designed to take your full weight when you're ripping their clothes off in a torrid frenzy in the kitchen? I'd be very wary of anyone who is determined to keep reality checks in place when it comes to matters of love. After all, a little bit of fantasy does you good.

do u believe in love at first sight? or i should walk by again?

Is this how Michael Jackson developed the moonwalk?

bincoculars, but will immediately go into a cheesy but strangely alluring derobing dance that you will find hypnotic. Failing that, we just call and rendez vous... your call...

June 13 at 2:04am

I love the way you twist about words to your liking. they dance a little two step of slang and metaphor and create a jazz production of meanings. I have great adoration for fizzy new slang and squeal inside whenever I hear new ones. I really must get some Hackney rhyming slang under my belt- but really that stuff is almost impossible to interpret along. Hah! God your so funny!! Completely my taste of humor down to an art. The beautiful weaving of ridiculous tales that go on in a dry wit manor. La sigh... (hearts and stars and twinkly lights!!)
I'll write you again tonight with the official logistics.

> subject>

Take care sweet word prince
B

Talk about competitive love note writing! This reads like some sort of face off between Shakespeare and Byron. Who can write the most poetic poignant prose EVER! I'm like, *so* going to out love you. This guy isn't going to be satisfied with being called the 'word prince', goddamnit, he wants to be the word king, yes, king I say!

I guess the written word becomes much more important when you can't see each other. This conversation took place through a social networking site, where the pair met. (When printed out this conversation was seventy-two – yes, seventy-two – pages long).
It seems to be working out between these two, but there are some definite issues with trying to match-make on the Internet, the main one being the potential for lying, or at the very least massaging the truth. Just when you think you've met the love of your life, you find out you have been flirting with a balding OAP with a bit of time on their hands. Also, you often have to summarise yourself in fifteen words or less, which can be a little tricky. In fact if it isn't, you either don't have much to say about yourself or your name says it all (e.g. Brad Pitt).
I haven't yet worked out if there really are any famous sex symbols using social networks. Rumour has it that the likes of Jennifer Aniston and Kylie use them to escape fame hunters and meet 'normal' people. I don't advise trying to chat with 'Brad Pitt' if you find him online; 'he' is probably a bored pensioner in Derby.

To the ~~[name]~~ ~~[scratched]~~ (who ~~[xxx]~~ still owes me something)

I promised to write a ~~[x]~~ note so I thought would now. I don't really know how to put into words how exactly I came to feel this strongly again and how much I want you back but I promise that Ill try in the next subtle way somewhere in this wee note. {I'm such a big sap} Here we go straight to the mushy soppy staugh.

Sometimes (more like, always) when I'm thinking of you I just wish I could be with again, get another chance and make things write. Although things are very different at the moment and my chances slim I just hope that you will consider be as a factor and hopefully take my poor, innocent, little, lonely soul and excite it. I know it would work this time because (and I know that I've said it before) I really don't care for ~~[x]~~ anymore, I'm over this mountain after 1 year and 8½ months of climbing and my whole focus point is becomes focusing on only one guy, guess who? Yes you! You better write back.

Love   ~ x
         xx

P.S. Yes it is the usual conclusion.

[handwritten note in top right, pointing to "note"] Know ~ or what? ~ mean jelly bean

This is a big please, a pretty please. I hope the recipient managed to see past the dodgy backward sloping writing and the even more dodgy spelling. I don't quite know what the author means by making things write, though they do say at the end they are expecting a letter in return. Maybe they simply want a pen pal. Yes, let's hope that the recipient got past all these little issues and the small issue of the sender knowing exactly how long (to the day) it's been since they split up with their ex. I'm not quite sure they want to get together for all the write reasons.

> >>
> >>> From:
> >>> To: oonagh
> >>> Date:
> >>>
> >>> " I don't know what
did to deserve you saying good morning and good night to me every day, but if I knew I would do it again and again, you make my day and
you make my dreams sweeter"
> >>>
> >>>
> >>>
> >>>
> >>>
> > >>

This shows how unromantic I am, as I always find the lack of
punctuation in this text message confusing. I'm yet to receive a love
letter that has been sent back with red pen corrections and marks
out of ten. That said, if you added a 'see me' at the end of the letter
it would be a good excuse for a 'one to one' lesson!

You have always been the women whom I have loved,
even before we met I loved you in my dreams,
now you are more than just in my dreams,
you are my dreams...

Another whole lotta dreaming going on here.

--Forwarded Message Attachment--
Subject:
Date: ~~~~~~~~~~ 18:48:45 +0100
From:
To:

Come home x xx

I love you x x x

From:
Sent:
To:
Subject:

Like cherry pie? Love you too x

--Forwarded Message Attachment--
Subject:
Date:
From:
To:

With custard. X x x

For goodness' sake! This happens to the best of us, doesn't it? We start sounding as though we've been stuck in a rubbish greeting card shop, using terms like sugar bum, wobbly bits, cutie, ad nauseam. What is it about love that makes comedy names acceptable? I suppose it's fine in private or as pillow talk, but you wouldn't want anyone to see it in a book now, would you …

You may only be one person to the world, but you may also be the world to one person.

This is the sort of fortune cookie you would be happy to receive on a date (see page 30). Apparently you can also get one that says, 'that wasn't chicken you ate ...'

FORGIVE AND FORGET LOVE

I love you. No, *I* love *you*! I'm so sorry, I promise, I will, I do.
This section is for anyone out there who's willing to put your
differences to one side, kiss and make up, forgive and forget,
and make a promise for the future …

Heyalp, heyalp! Is this a note from Penelope Pitstop, or a line from Sue Ellen to JR? I desperately want this note to have been written by some glamour puss with shoulder pads and frosted hair. Preferably just before they deliver a faux slap and leave a motel grabbing their fur coat. It is a 1980s love note ... you baystard!

APPLICATION FOR A NIGHT OUT WITH THE BOYS

Name of Boyfriend/Fiancé/Husband: ▪▪▪▪▪▪▪▪

I request permission for a leave of absence from the **highest authority** in my life for the following period.

Date: `10.05.08` Time of departure: `06.40L` Time of return `N/A` NOT to exceed *Pref: relevat ef my ulesses is his late...*

Should permission be granted, I do solemnly swear to only visit the locations stated below, at the stated times. I agree to refrain from hitting on or flirting with other women. I shall not even speak to another female, except as expressly permitted in writing below. I will not turn off my mobile after two pints, nor shall I consume above the allowed volume of alcohol without first phoning for a taxi AND calling you for a verbal waiver of said alcohol allowance. I understand that even if permission is granted to go out, my girlfriend/fiancé/wife retains the right to be pissed off with me the following week for no valid reason whatsoever.

Amount of alcohol allowed (units) Beer ☐ Wine ☐ Liquor ☐ Total ☐
unlimited

Locations to be visited	Location:	From: To:
	Location: `N/A`	From: To:
	Location:	From: To:

Females with whom conversation is permitted: *Use your judgement. Try to ask yourself "what would ... say if he ...? Most females al... are permitted (if by speak intelligible English)*

IMPORTANT – STRIPPER CLAUSE: Not withstanding the female contact permitted above, I promise to refrain from coming within one hundred (100) feet of a stripper or exotic dancer. Violation of this Stripper Clause shall be grounds for <u>immediate termination of</u> the relationship.

I acknowledge my position in life. I know who wears the trousers in our relationship, and I agree it's not me. I promise to abide by your rules & regulations. I understand that this is going to cost me a fortune in chocolates & flowers. You reserve the right to obtain and use my credit cards whenever you wish to do so. I hereby promise to take you on an unlimited shopping spree should I not return home by the approved time. On my way home, I will not pick a fight with any stranger, nor shall I conduct in depth discussions with the said entity. Upon my return home, I promise not to urinate anywhere other than in the toilet. In addition, I will refrain from waking you up, breathing my vile breath in your face, and attempting to breed like a (drunken) rabbit.

I declare that to the best of my knowledge (of which I have none compared to my **BETTER** half), the above information is correct.
Signed – Boyfriend/Fiancé/Husband ▪▪▪▪▪▪▪ ▪▪▪▪▪▪▪

Request is: APPROVED ☑ **DENIED** ☐

This decision is not negotiable. If approved, cut permission slip below and carry at all times.
✂- -
Permission for my boyfriend/fiancé/husband to be away for the following period of time:
Date: `10.05.08` Time of departure: `06.40` Time of return: `N/A`

Signed – Girlfriend/Fiancé/Wife ▪▪▪▪▪▪▪▪

A very wise (and now married) young lady submitted this. A pre-nup's one thing, but a pre-stag do agreement is genius. If I knew who had created this form, I would credit them. To be honest, if he quibbles over any of the points on the list, then you should probably quit while you're ahead – complaints about not being given permission to sleep with a hooker and acquire an STD just before your wedding night are definitely a bad omen.

Stag and hen dos are all a bit weird, and recently they've become increasingly confusing. In some countries a hen do is known as a 'stagette' or 'bachelorette' do, politically correct terms which seem a bit ironic when you're about to go out blowing your willy whistles.

Sorry I have
had to go to work
will call later —
By the way. ya
Still look
gorgeous with sick
on yourself (hee he)
∴
—x—

Nooooooo! It can't be true. You spent time, money and effort trying to look like hot stuff for your date. The last thing you remember is downing a lot of Dutch courage, and possibly a kebab? Then you wake up panda-eyed on the sofa, wondering what the funny smell is. That'll be the sick all over your frock, love. How did you get back? Oh yes, your lovely new suitor made sure you got home safely. This is a good initiation test actually – if they can love you in that state they're probably a good bet.

This is a blurry picture of a message scrawled on the wall of a club. I guess some of the great writers of our time came up with some of their most poignant prose under the influence of opium, so it should come as no surprise that after five energy drinks and vodka someone was hit with this startling yet beautiful revelation. Just don't ask them to remember it in the morning.

SELFLESS LOVE

I would do anything for love, really. This is the selfless,
'no, please, after you' love. This is the 'please take my money
and my drugs and my heart while you're at it' section, where the
authors are willing to walk over hot coals to reach their loved one.

I don't know. You put your criminal record, possibly your life, and definitely your street cred, on the line by trying to be cool, calm and collected while striking a deal with some unsavoury character for whatever drug you desire. And how do you get thanked? By having it taken off you before you've even had a chance to make a fool of yourself in some bad nightclub, thinking you're the world's greatest dancer and that you love everyone in the whole sweaty place. It must be love if you let them take your Class As.

I've had a horrid thought about this. I hope the drugs in question weren't an asthma/angina/diabetes prescription. Have two lives been put at risk in a crazy attempt to get high on insulin ... oh God, why can't everyone just sit at home drinking cocoa?

Good Luck Have A Lovely
Day. I Love you More
Than Anything. I Love
Your Hair.
Love .u.
Your BeefCAKE
xxxxx

Take Care Today

264

This dude has got it sussed. He knows how to win any lady over. Not with the 'I love you more than anything' comment, which is a bit extreme, but with the 'I love your hair' line. There's nothing worse than placing a huge amount of importance on a change like this and then realising it has achieved nothing. Whether it's a change of location, attitude, or hair, if it has had zero impact then you're in the same zone you were in before.

For example, I once bought a leotard after watching a Cindy Crawford workout video. (I watched it too many times to be healthy for my own mental state. I didn't do the exercises, mind, just sat there eating toast.) The leotard she was wearing somehow became the answer to all my body-image and exercise issues. Basically, I morphed from thinking, 'Maybe if I get some wacky clothes to exercise in, I will suddenly enjoy exercising ... ' to, 'If I get a leotard I may even grow a body, if not a face, like Cindy Crawford!' I wore it once to a 'step' class and spent the whole time worrying that my bum was wobbling so much it was about to start clapping. It's fair to say the change in attire didn't bring the magical results I'd hoped for.

The effect of a new hair-do can also be blown out of all proportion, of course. Will it take years off you? Will it make you look classic or funky? Or will it just make you neurotic? To have nobody notice can be hugely deflating, which is why a finely tuned man must have written this note. He knew that the comment wasn't so much about the hair itself, but making sure the nut job *with* the hair feels great for the rest of the day. As much as I would like to think that my haircut is for my own benefit, if I thought somebody actively liked, or even loved it, I could definitely start to believe that they must love *me* a lot.

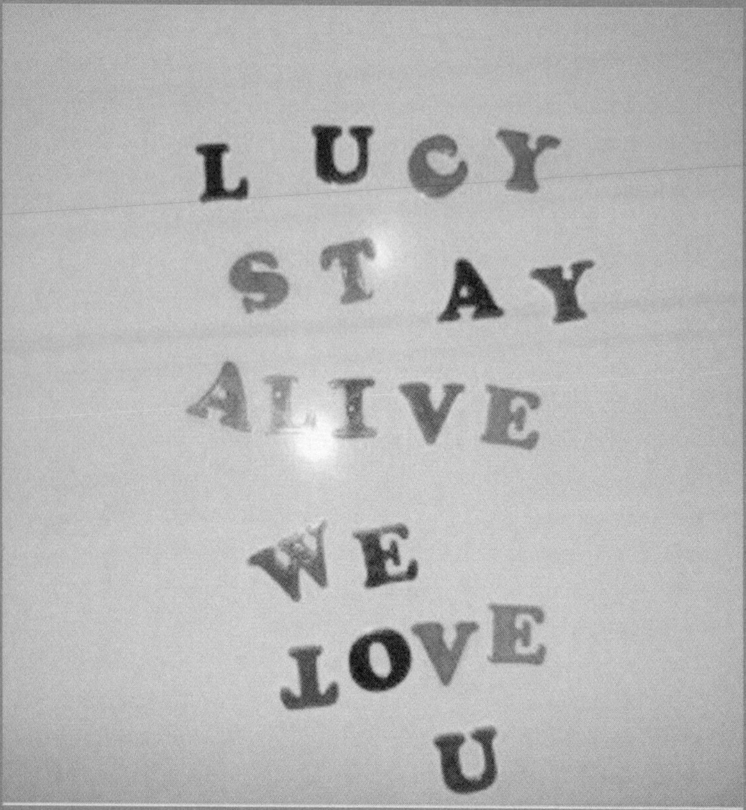
LUCY
STAY
ALIVE
WE
LOVE
U

How lovely to be loved. As this is on a fridge rather than in a card (and the premise of this book is that it is meant to be light hearted), I presume that Lucy isn't really close to death. If she is, then writing this note in comedy magnetic letters on a fridge seems more than a little sick in the head.

Having said that, it *has* given me a fantastic idea. If … sorry … *when* I die, I could perhaps get a metal casket and my family and friends could use these magnets to write all sorts of happy, loving messages on my coffin. Although I guess I'd be a little concerned that my family might get carried away, in the way that those middle-class poetry magnets you can buy become rude haikus after a few weeks of trying to be grown-up. On second thoughts, perhaps I'll give it a miss.

I get a lot of notes from students, so I can only hope that Lucy has been cramming for exams too late, or been partying too hard.

> P.S. I WILL WASH UP
> WHEN I GET
> BACK... -
>
> HONEY,
> I LOVE YOU
> V. MUCH. HAVE
> A LOVELY TIME
> TONIGHT
> I AM SO PROUD
> OF YOU
> . xxxxxx

Oh yeah, another bribe. It's all well and good to tell someone how much you love them and how great they are as a stand-alone statement, but with a p.s., an if, or a but, it becomes a bit lame. Looks like emotional blackmail is the new vogue. I love you so much I couldn't be bothered donning the old Marigolds and doing the washing up? How disappointing. Thinking this through you might start to wonder, 'If they love me so much but can't be arsed to do the washing up, what happens if I get hit by a bus and end up in a wheelchair? Will they just leave me there with the brake on for hours on end, or will they leave me full stop? A small, flippant comment such as 'Yes, I'll do that later' or 'I promise' can really escalate if you're, er, well, me.

If I become pure pan bread (dead)
by the way . . . get all
my stuff n' that. That my
last will and testament

(unless he (. . .) kills
me then . . . gets
everythg) –

There are thousands of things outside of money and possessions that can be offered in a relationship. Judging by this makeshift will, the author doesn't have much to offer, but at least they can provide some humour. If you can make someone laugh – even after an argument – maybe they are exactly right for you after all.

Afterword

And I'm spent. How was it for you? Personally, I'm exhausted. I'm pleased to say we went through the good times and the bad together. If you only remember the good times in your relationships, you'd end up going out with everyone you have ever dated (which just sounds complicated to me). The one thing that this book has taught me is that we should just keep moving onwards and upwards. Don't be tempted to rewind, go back, or look over your shoulder: just learn from your mistakes and try not to repeat or regret.

I should also take this opportunity to thank some people (apart from family, friends and exes!): as ever, Gordon Wise at Curtis Brown, Jonny at Trunk Records, www.garudiostudiage.com, Mark, Dean and Helen. Especially Antonia Hodgson, Adam Strange, Kirsteen Astor, Hannah Boursnell, Melissa Rudd and everyone at Little, Brown who have not only been fantastic to work with, but have put up with me harassing them for their own love stories. I should also thank them for not laughing too loud at my own stories of love and love lost. Also, thanks to all of those people out there who visit www.flatmatesanonymous.com and have added notes and have generally got involved. I hope to keep the relationship going.
Before I forget, I should also thank those people who are so vain they probably think this book is about them. I have had a very enjoyable time looking at all your notes, relationships and love from every angle – some angles being more flattering than others. It is a relief to see that nobody has found it plain sailing. Even those who talk about 'the one' and how 'they just knew' seem to just edit out the bits that they don't think fit into their love story. That's fine; whatever floats your boat. Actually, I've also found out that quite a lot of things seem to float your boats, from inanimate objects to men with beards. There is something for everyone out there. In the words of a true Lothario, you can't always get what you want, but you might find you get what you need. So whether

you got this book as a gift, gave it to someone for Valentine's Day, or bought it to cheer yourself up after a dodgy break up, I hope it has fulfilled your needs … and that you got everything that you wanted from it.